THINKING CHRISTIAN
Essays on Testimony, Accountability, and the Christian Mind

JAMES SPENCER, PhD

Copyright © 2020
James Spencer, PhD
Thinking Christian
Essays on Testimony, Accountability, and the Christian Mind
All rights reserved.

No part of this publication may be reproduced, distributed, or transmitted in any form or by any means, including photocopying, recording, or other electronic or mechanical methods, without the prior written permission of the publisher, except in the case of brief quotations embodied in critical reviews and certain other non-commercial uses permitted by copyright law.

James Spencer, PhD

Printed in the United States of America
First Printing 2020
First Edition 2020

10 9 8 7 6 5 4 3 2 1

To my amazing, supportive wife, my kids for whom I strive to leave a godly legacy, my church that shapes my understanding of God, and my friends and colleagues who pursue God with tenacity.

"…Be infants in evil, but in your thinking be mature."

1 Corinthians 14:20

Table of Contents

1 Introduction 1
2 The Christian Mind 7
3 Christian Thought In A World Of Excess 25
4 Cultivating A Christian Mind 41
5 Public Christian Testimony 61
6 Responsible Christian Testimony 77
7 Christians And Power 93
8 Terrible Simplification 121
9 Accountability In Fresh Perspective 139
10 Theology As Path Dependent 163
11 Conclusion 175
Acknowledgments 179
Endnotes 181

1 Introduction

Early in my career I found myself in a situation in which, my denominational outsider status and, I'm sure, a variety of other factors, resulted in a rather tense "interview" with a small, Southern Baptist Association in central Illinois. I was applying to a Director of Missions (DOM) position and needed the association to "confirm my calling" to the job. As I was beginning to field questions during the association meeting, one of the pastors stood up and proclaimed that he didn't want anyone in the DOM position that "would not bleed for the Southern Baptist faith." Once the chorus of "Amen" died down, it became quite clear that not being a member of the denomination would mean that my call would not be confirmed.

Coming out of that experience, I began to write and reflect on the role that God is given in our communities and organizations. Thankfully, none of those reflections were ever published. It was an act of grace on God's part to keep my thoughts from that point in my life confined to my hard drive. Reading back over the essays I wrote at that time, I have been pleased to find that they contain some solid theological insights (insights I believe I have enhanced in the essays that follow). Yet, while revisiting my early musings, it is quite clear that the angry young man who wrote them needed to have far more grace, humility, and patience. More than a decade later, having been blessed to encounter women and men who were willing to push and challenge me to embody the theology I have worked so hard to learn, I am excited to revisit some of the themes from my unpublished work with a more humble, less ambitious, vindictive spirit.

During my time in leadership at Moody Bible Institute in Chicago (MBI), I learned a great deal about who I am as a leader and a person. Many of those lessons have come into greater focus since I left. To use a weight training analogy: muscles break down when you lift heavy objects…they heal and become stronger when given time outside the gym to rest. I have found there is a similar dynamic involved in developing Christian character and in cultivating Christian thought. The challenges of life offer the tension and "weight" necessary to strengthen our character and clarify our thinking. Being able to reflect on what was a rather challenging leadership experience, particularly in the last two or three years at MBI, without the pressures to increase enrollment, reduce budget, play politics, or jockey for resources, has been enriching.

This book is, to some extent, my attempt to reflect theologically on some of the questions with which I've wrestled during the first phase of my career. I've tried to address questions I don't believe we, as the body of Christ, have done enough to answer. Primary among those questions is what it means to develop a "Christian mind." As the community of faith seeks to navigate an environment that is differently complex than those of previous eras, we need a Christian mind capable of confronting the challenges we face both in our local and, increasingly, digital communities.

I have a love/hate relationship with the digital world. I recently started a website (nextgenchristians.com) where I offer occasional perspectives on issues I'm thinking about and which (I hope) are relevant to the church and its individual members. I follow a number of fitness professionals on Instagram, listen to a few select podcasts, watch interviews on YouTube, purchase books on Amazon, and keep up with friends and family on Facebook. Despite its shortcomings, the digital age has brought with it the potential to connect women and men around the world, to highlight local perspectives, and to provide platforms for those whose voices might otherwise go unheard.

New digital technologies have taken on a life of their own. Even after the so-called "dot.com bubble" burst in the early 2000's, digital companies like Google, Amazon, and Facebook emerged to give us hope of a new era of searching, shopping, and liking. As impressive and, often times, beneficial as these new technologies are, we cannot go on using them as if there are no adverse effects to having virtually instantaneous access to information, elevating impulse buying to an art form, and amassing friends with the click of a button.

As a Christian community testifying to the God who sent His Son to die for sinners and gave us the Holy Spirit to guide us into all truth, we do not have the luxury of naively ignoring the dark side of the digital age. At the same time, we cannot place the blame for the woes we face as a Christian community on the rise of the internet. The digital age has enhanced certain dynamics within the Christian community, but those dynamics…the underlying patterns of thought, interaction, and authority…were forming and shaping the Christian community well before anyone "got mail."

While some dangers, like pornography, are painfully apparent in our new digital environment, I am more concerned that those who proclaim "Jesus is Lord" have not reckoned with what it means to offer faithful Christian testimony in a digital age. My concern is that we have developed a way of thinking about God, the world, and the manner in which we exist within it without engaging in sufficiently deep theological reflection.[1] At the same time, when we have not offered a faithful digital presence, it is, in part, because we did not have a good idea of what it meant to offer a faithful "analog" presence.

We have brought some bad habits with us into the digital age…ways of thinking and acting that are more divisive than unifying and more vindictive than redemptive. The digital age and its tools, then, are not so much the culprit, but the mechanism by which our collective mis-thinking regarding a number of matters has become more evident. We must take greater care to get down to the true roots of our problem…to the more fundamental theological errors that distort our understanding of the way we embody Christ in the world.

Mass media has not always aided the body of Christ's public testimony. Some of those who have a more national or international voice seem hell bent on being agitators instead of a calming presence. Some seem quite content to offer thin theological arguments focused on a narrow set of issues that tend to dominate our collective conversations (at least online).

At the same time, there seems to be less willingness to reflect on the manner in which evangelicalism's own internal dynamics have contributed to divisiveness and animosity within the Christian community. I am not suggesting that prominent evangelical leadership is solely or even primarily responsible for divisions within the community or for the distortion of the gospel by those who, having had bad experiences in the church, have thrown God away as well. Rather, I am suggesting that it is shortsighted to assume that churches and their leaders (even those who would be considered "faithful") have not added fuel (even if inadvertently) to some of the fires we currently face.

Throughout the following essays, I seek to delve more deeply into some of the more fundamental dynamics that seem to be holding the church back from embodying a faithful testimony. I will admit that my own background and experience have tended to skew my concerns toward matters related to the life of the mind, to questions of ecclesiology, and to Christian testimony (in word and deed) though I also see the need for reevaluating accountability and the Christian use of power. As such, several of the essays included in this volume deal with matters related to discourse and "speech" (whether written or spoken).

If we take seriously biblical statements about speech and the tongue (Prov 6:16-19; Jer 9:3-5; Matt 12:34; Lk 6:45; James 1:26; 3:5; 1 Peter 3:10), about the nature of pure religion (James 1:27), and about truth and love within the community of faith (1 John 2:1-6;), I believe we will find it difficult to justify the sort of public testimony to which we seem to have become accustomed. Whether it be the uncareful musings of certain Christian authors, bloggers, and speakers, our collective tolerance of authoritarian leadership, or the anxieties and agendas of the community that distort the mission of the church, the Christian community needs to rediscover God and allow Him to reshape us so that we can witness to God's reign in the midst of a world in need of redemption.

The essays that follow hang together but are not necessarily dependent on each other. As such, they could be read in just about any order with one exception. The chapter entitled "The Christian Mind" is a more foundational essay that informs much of my thinking in the other essays. It was the first essay written and I would recommend reading it first. I have tried to arrange the essays in a logical order, but they need not be read sequentially. My hope is that these essays will contribute to a conversation that needs to be had within evangelicalism.

As a community, we need to learn to please God together. The only way for us to do so is to rethink the ways we relate to one another, how we structure our relationships, and what it means to be a people that offers faithful Christian testimony.

2 The Christian Mind

My family and I moved to Chicago in 2012. My son was seven at the time and had, up to that point, not lived in the city. He had grown up in a small town in Central Illinois where the buildings are shorter, the traffic slower, and the people fewer. These differences became particularly evident when my son and I were shopping on Michigan Avenue. Having grown up downstate, my son was not used to walking close to me. On the relatively empty sidewalks of Carlinville, IL, he could run to the next corner and wait for me…he didn't have to stay by my side. A crowded Michigan Avenue, however, brings new challenges.

I watched as my son tried to navigate the bustling Chicago sidewalks on his own. He was being jostled and bumped out of the way by walkers who didn't notice him. He dodged groups of shoppers, backtracked to avoid people guilty of texting while walking, and hugged the walls to avoid being trampled. I watched him for a bit before calling him over to walk closer to me. At the time, I was 6 ft, 250 lbs with about 3/4 of my right arm covered by tattoos. People saw me coming. I didn't bully my way through the crowds, but I wasn't exactly dodging every walker either. At my side, my son was able to walk more confidently. He didn't have to dip, duck, dive, and dodge. He benefited from my physical stature and presence and was able to walk as if he was also 6ft, 250 lbs. He walked differently because he walked with me.

Just as my son walked differently next to me, so Christians can live, move, and (most importantly for the purposes of this essay) think differently because is with us. While "worldview" has become a rather fashionable ...tian worldview is not the star of the Christian drama. The Christian worldview is important but thinking Christianly is not solely a question of having a useful story about the world around us, but of imagining rightly the manner in which we interact with God and others. This imagining is described by Taylor as a "social imaginary" which is:

> "…something much broader and deeper than the intellectual schemes people may entertain when they think about social reality in a disengaged mode. I am thinking, rather, of the ways people imagine their social existence, how they fit together with others, how things go on between them and their fellows, the expectations that are normally met, and the deeper normative notions and images that underlie these expectations."[2]

While Taylor does not reference God as a social actor, God is a social being interacting with us as the most prominent member of our community. As such, the social imaginary of the "Christian mind" is not simply one that considers the social existence of humans with humans.[3] It also recognizes God with us in the world he has created.

The space God has created is strongly connected to identity and contributes to the variegated nature of the body of Christ and our theological conceptualizations.[4] Displacement and abstraction, arguably a major challenge in a digital age, pull us away from a local world in which God is at work in diverse and distinct ways. Our social existence with God and humanity within a specific space is made intelligible through the text of Scripture, the illumination of the Holy Spirit, and the historical and contemporary discourses of the Christian community.

God and Community

Given that God is the most prominent member of our community whose presence dwells with us through the Holy Spirit, the manner in which we imagine our social existence differs from those who do not recognize God and do not participate in the ongoing, cross-generational discourse of the community of faith. We are not simply a community in the present, but a community with long, situated histories all of which contribute to the multi-layered testimony offered by the unified body of Christ.[5] As we remember that history from the standpoint of our present circumstances, the past and the present interact to develop the church's "sense of itself as a continuous entity through time, as well as to the manifestations of, and efforts to enhance, that sense of community."[6]

Our sense of community as the body of Christ is rooted in our understanding of God and our relationship with him. The scriptures reveal God and serve as the final authority and "norming norm" for life and faith providing the paradigms and frameworks for faithful imagination. The community of faith is tethered to the canon of Scripture and cannot offer a "sense of community" or imagine a social existence with God and others that runs against the grain of the text.

The scriptures do not confine the church to an archaic mode of life that rejects progress. Instead, the scriptures represent the "living and active" word of God that guides the community of faith providing the resources needed to navigate ever-changing contexts while maintaining a clear, communal identity through time. In this sense, the biblical canon may be understood as a mnemonic event which conditions the collective remembering of the community of faith. It is largely, though not solely, through the scriptures that the community's collective remembering is forged and the church's cross-generational identity maintained.

God also participates in the formation of memory through the illuminating work of the Holy Spirit. The testimony of faith is influenced, for better or worse, by the space and time in which the community of faith negotiates its past and present. The community of faith is situated, temporal, and, thus, lacking a universal, fully objective perspective on its social existence. The Spirit works on the individual and collective mind of the community of faith so that we are enabled "to receive what the Spirit's inspired scriptures say as meaningful and, in fact, authoritative for our own thinking and acting…the fact that we receive the word of God as the guiding authority for our lives informs the ongoing development of our pre-understanding for approaching the biblical text anew."[7]

The Holy Spirit works in individual members of the faith community and amongst the community as a whole guiding and shaping not only the behavior of the community, but the way we imagine our social existence. As Hauerwas notes, "The Holy Spirit works to help us find one another so that we will not suffer the fears and anxieties that fuel the violence derived from being alone. To be so located is to discover that God invites us to share his very life found in Jesus of Nazareth. For it turns out the principle work of the Holy Spirit…is to point to Jesus."[8]

The past, present, and future community of faith engages in its ongoing, situated discourses across time in the presence of God and in deep interactions with God's word. This communal discourse is not limited to academics, to the great works of Christian theology, or to popular preachers or authors. The whole Christian community contributes to the collective remembering and the negotiation of identity from past to present as it engages in the aspects essential to Christian theology. As Vanhoozer notes, "To be a Christian theologian is to seek, speak, and show understanding of what God was doing in Christ for the sake of the world."[9] That the whole community of faith practices theology is not trivial. We often default to the assumption that those with big ministries or academic credentials are the theologians. When we mistake credentials for character or the accessibility and popularity of a given work with its ability to convey truth, we forget the vital function of everyday acts.[10]

While various technologies and structures have provided a context for the development and distribution of influential theological work in the Western world, the tomes written by the likes of Augustine, Calvin, Luther, Barthes, and others only *contribute* to a global, historic discourse…they do not *define* it or set its limits. These and other works do not overshadow or dominate the whole theological testimony of God's people, yet neither are they to be silenced simply because they do not comprehensively address the theological expressions or experiences of Christian communities they do not represent.[11]

The community of faith does not silence new voices, it negotiates, engages in discourse, and draws provisional conclusions that are subjected to the scriptures. Vanhoozer's comments are instructive:

> "…tradition enjoys the authority that attaches to the testimony of many witnesses. In this light, we may view the church fathers and church councils as expert witnesses as to the sense of Scripture in the courtroom drama of doctrine. Neither the Fathers nor the councils sit on the bench; the triune God has the final say. The task of theology is to cross-examine the witnesses in order to offer proximate judgements under the ultimate authority of residing judge: the Spirit speaking in the scriptures."[12]

The Christian Mind

Given this brief sketch of God and community, there are three points that may be identified as crucial to any description of the Christian mind. **First**, we are social beings whose imagined social existence impacts the way we interact with God, humanity, and the rest of creation. We develop a sense through which we understand how God, humans, and the rest of creation interact, what "expectations are normally met" in those interactions, and "the deeper normative notions and images that underlie these expectations."[13] In short, as the body of Christ, we have our own peculiar social imaginary. As individual social beings this social imaginary is not conjured up through an autonomous act. Instead, "the conscience of the individual members of a community is a repository of the moral understanding which shaped it, and may serve to perpetuate it in a crisis of collapsing morale or institution."[14]

Second, we are not simply applying a rigid framework of rules and principles, but are a remembering community striving to retain continuity with the faith community of the past. We are not above time and history, nor do we have a universal perspective. We are a situated community linking arms with generations past (and leaving a legacy for future generations). We must negotiate the complex web of the present while honoring and remaining connected with those who came before us. Surely there are enduring expectations and "normative notions" that transcend generations; however, the dynamics involved in social existence in the past and present are not static, which leaves us to negotiate past and present as we seek to engage in faithful collective remembering together.[15]

Finally, we do not imagine our social existence without limits. We are a people in communion with God whose ongoing work in our lives allows us to recognize the text of Scripture as the "norming norm" and final authority for life and faith. Our imaginations will be judged in light of the full message of the scriptures. Christian imagination must render the vastness of the Triune God faithfully. Truthfulness does not take precedence over the redemptive intention of Christian speech, nor does kindness trump our responsibility to speak difficult, truthful words. Academic discourse is not an excuse for excessive critique or the demeaning of Christian brothers and sisters, nor is the banner of journalism, the mantra of free speech, or the quest for justice a license to defame one another in public. We are an imaginative, cross-generational, global community called by God and guided by the Spirit and the scriptures striving to situate ourselves faithfully in the concrete settings in which we find ourselves. As Welch notes, "…the church has no existence as immanent historical community independent of God calling it and sustaining it in being."[16]

Characteristics of the Christian Mind

Having offered a thumbnail sketch of the dynamics involved in imagining our social existence as a community of faith in an ongoing relationship with God, it is now time to consider the Christian mind. The Christian mind emerges from our imagined social existence in so much as it is influenced by a combination of elements and constrained by (a) God's ongoing activity in our individual and collective lives, (b) the "norming norm" of Scripture, and (c) the inter-generational discourse of the faithful in which we participate. The Christian mind is not simply a product of our own individual musings or values, but a mind forged in the comfort and crucible of Christian community. In fact, the Christian mind is not only an individual mind at all, but a broader mode of analysis…a disposition toward the world embodied by the community of faith as a whole.

While any list of characteristics is likely to be lacking, there are at least eight associated with a Christian mind. These eight characteristics are not listed in order of hierarchy, nor should it be assumed that they create a harmonious framework in which Christian thought may be easily produced. Instead, the characteristics will, at times, stand in tension with one another requiring discernment, wisdom, and the courage that comes from knowing that our decisions, while important, are never as consequential as we would like to think.

First, the Christian mind is a connected, not an isolated, mind. It is shaped by God within and for the body of Christ. The Christian mind develops through the church's faithful participation with God, ongoing meditation on the scriptures, the church's doctrines, works of theology, and thoughtful engagement with the outside world and the critics of the faith. The Christian mind cannot flourish within an echo chamber that only reinforces predominant perspectives and approaches to the Christian life. Developing a Christian mind is impossible outside of communion with God in Christ. It will also remain incomplete without a body of Christ whose members together navigate the present and seek to faithfully render God in continuity with past generations of the faithful.

When we are separate from other members of the body of Christ, we are lacking. Perhaps we are not lacking so severely that we are unable to think Christianly, but we are lacking just the same. We are incomplete…having realized less of our potential than we might…because we have yet to encounter the faith of other members of Christ's body. Here Paul's statement in Romans 1:11-12 is instructive: "For I long to see you, that I may impart to you some spiritual gift to strengthen you—that is, that we may be mutually encouraged by each other's faith, both yours and mine." Paul recognizes the reciprocal benefit available within the Christian community asserting his confidence that he will bring a "spiritual gift" while acknowledging his need for the encouragement that comes through interactions within the rest of the community. Paul is lacking without the benefit he will receive from the

Romans. He is different without them and they without him. The Christian mind embraces this notion of interdependence and reciprocity finding ways to strengthen the body of Christ through the interactions of its members.

Second, the Christian mind is a situated mind. It is situated within the complex matrix of social life. It is not ahistorical or abstracted, but embedded within the ongoing environments in which God's people find themselves. There is certainly continuity across ages and generations. It is not that the church is unrecognizable from one era to the next. Without denying the enduring, immutable character of God and His word or the necessity of stable doctrine, the Christian mind embraces the negotiations between "remembered pasts and constructed presents" that constitute the process of collective remembering.[17]

This negotiation honors not just the scriptures, but those who have negotiated their own present (our past), thought Christianly, and contributed to the ongoing collective remembering of the community. The Christian mind does not deny absolute truth, nor does it argue that truth is somehow relative and subject to the whims and limitations of humankind. Instead, the Christian mind understands its limits and location, as well as the limits and location of those who have thought Christianly in the past. It is a situated mind not because of any prior epistemological commitment, but because we experience our transcendent, atemporal, and infinite God within space and time as temporal, finite beings.

Because the Christian mind understands its own limitations, it remains humble, gracious, and open to different configurations of Christian thought. The human mind cannot fully account for all of the complexities of the social world, nor does it need to do so. Instead, to think Christianly is not to see rightly at every moment, but to remain pliable and open to correction and critique. The Christian mind acknowledges contribution, laments error and the perversion of the truth, and seeks to stand on the flawed and faithful shoulders of other Christian thinkers.

It is important to note that the past itself is pliable because additional faithful expressions from the past may always be taken into account. Take, for instance, the manner in which Stephen reorients and conveys what appears to be a neglected point about God's activity within Israel. God was never confined to the land of Israel, but appeared to Abraham in Mesopotamia (Acts 7:2), was with Israel in Egypt (7:9-36), and moved with His people in the tabernacle until Solomon built the temple (7:44-47). While Stephen does not deny the significance of the temple, he does remind those listening (those who would soon stone him) that God is not confined to the temple (7:48-49). By framing the history of Israel in too rigid a fashion, Stephen's audience was unwilling to acknowledge all that God was doing in the world (7:51-53).

While the Western theological tradition has been more widely influential due to a number of technological and political factors, the Western tradition does not represent the full theological testimony of the church. The closure of the canon and the broad, inter-generational consensus regarding core doctrines provide boundaries for negotiation, but they do not constrain movement completely. The Christian mind is no longer Christian if it dismisses the scriptures as the "norming norm" or finally denies the core doctrines of the historic Christian community. The Christian mind must take care not to "resist the Holy Spirit" (7:51) by representing that our particular understanding of the scriptures or of God more generally is somehow less situated and more universal than warranted.

No situated treatment of the biblical text offers a full and complete account. As such, the "remembered past" may be expanded and re-negotiated in the present as new insights from or about the past are incorporated into the broader tradition. In other words, I cannot deny Luther a place simply because my tradition emphasizes Calvin. I cannot deny Cone's *The Cross and the Lynching Tree* simply because his voice disrupts what many assume to be settled, nor can we deny González's *Mañana* because he writes of theology from a Hispanic perspective.[18]

The consensus of the believing community is a bane and a blessing. Surely the collective wisdom of the people of God has benefited the church, such as in the formation of doctrinal positions. At the same time the consensus of the community of faith is not always formed with complete information and, as such, must be open to revision and ongoing negotiation on certain matters. The works of Luther, Calvin, Cone, and González are not without their shortcomings. The point is not that we have been ignoring a pristine theology that would correct all of our problems. Rather, the point is that what we see is not all there is. As such, we need to avoid framing the issues of theology too narrowly by ignoring voices outside of our traditions.

Recognizing the pliability of Christian thought and identifying the situated nature of God's word does not deny its ongoing significance or diminish its ability to convey transcendent truth. Rather, the text of Scripture reveals God through literary genres situated within a particular time, place, and culture. The stories, poems, prophecies, laws, and letters of the scriptures reveal a God who is beyond His creation (transcendent) even as he interacts with his creation (immanence). God's identity is not conveyed solely through assertion, but is demonstrated through particular experiences of God remembered by the community of faith. It is through these situated, culturally appropriate writings that the body of Christ today understands the character of God.

Third, the Christian mind is concerned with holistic testimony. Coady captures the concept well: "…it is plain that people who speak of the witness or the testimony of martyrs or the lives of men dedicated to certain ideals intend to convey by that language the idea that the words and deeds of the men (or women) in question stand to the 'realities' they believe in, rather as reports stand to the realities they are about."[19] The Christian mind, thus, recognizes that faithful testimony entails more than verbal or written affirmations about our imagined social existence with God, others, and the world around us. Faithful testimony encompasses actions and ways of life that point to individual and collective understandings.

For example, publicly bludgeoning other members of the community of faith in the pursuit of righteousness yields a muddled, partial testimony (and often mixed results). While others may now understand that the community of faith holds to a particular theological, political, or social position, they no longer see through our actions a patient, kind God committed to a unified body of Christ, nor do they see a community of which they would want to be a part. While the faithful testimony of the Christian community does not guarantee that unbelievers will flock to the church, faithful Christian testimony does need to be an expression of communal identity rooted in God's kingly rule.

As such, the Christian mind cannot seek to be right, or to come to the right conclusion on a given position, at any cost. Instead, the Christian mind is committed to coming to correct conclusions through Christlike discourse and acting on those conclusions in a manner that reflects the God we serve. Right doctrine is crucial to maintaining the boundaries of faithful Christian community.[20] However, the Christian mind recognizes that there is more to being faithful to such doctrines than intellectual agreement. Such doctrines have implications that require certain Christian action and ways of relating.

For instance, Paul states in his instructions to Titus, "Show yourself in all respects to be a model of good works, and in your teaching show integrity, dignity, and sound speech that cannot be condemned, so that an opponent may be put to shame, having nothing evil to say about us" (Titus 2:7-8). Note the shift from Paul's exhortation for Titus to be a model worthy of imitation to the communal implications of Titus's action in v. 8 ("…so that an opponent may be put to shame, having nothing evil to say about us"). Even as Paul urges Titus to rebuke false teachers and to address the behavior of those in his community, he reminds him that these activities are to be done in a manner commensurate with "sound doctrine" (2:1). It seems clear that Paul wants to highlight the mutually reinforcing nature of Christian behavior and Christian doctrine (cf. 2:9-10). Thinking with a Christian mind means acknowledging that right belief and right action are inseparable…that the manner in which we convey truth (not simply the truth itself) speaks to our own character and to the character of God.

Fourth, the Christian mind demands accountability. Accountability is not simply achieved through structural means. What is means for the Christian mind to demand accountability is more than a desire to see justice done. Rather, it is a recognition that confession of sin within community is essential to what it means to be the body of Christ (James 5:16; 1 John 1:9). The Christian mind does not demand accountability to achieve purity within the community. In demanding accountability, we do not seek to create a highly monitored police state in which God's people conform in order not to deal with the consequences of being caught. Rather, we demand accountability because we care for those within the body and desire to see God's grace enacted in the community of faith. In essence, accountability is a crucial means by which the body of Christ bears witness to and glorifies God.

Christian discourse is impossible without expectations and norms to which Christians who engage in discourse agree to adhere. While the standards of other fields such as academia, journalism, philosophy, or debate may be well and good, Christian discourse cannot conform to those standards alone, but will likely need to expand on and transcend such standards. The Christian mind, in other words, cannot allow academic or journalistic interests to set agendas, establish values, or otherwise supersede Christian identity.[21] While the Christian mind may engage in discourses within fields and arenas outside of the community of faith, care must be taken to ensure that the Christian mind remains Christian even as it adapts to be intelligible within a particular academic discipline or professional guild.

The Christian mind is never divorced from the community of faith, nor is it made to submit to the reigning logics of other disciplines (no matter how virtuous they may be). When a Christian speaks, he or she speaks as a member of the body of Christ and is, thus, accountable to the community of faith. Autonomy is a myth not because the individual is so formed by a collective that he or she loses any meaningful sense of agency and responsibility. It is a myth because being a member of the body of Christ forges an organic connection between the individual members of the body of Christ. We retain responsibility for our actions as individual agents while recognizing that we also represent the other members of the body (1 Cor. 12:12-31). We are individuals, but we are not isolated.

Fifth, the Christian mind rejects systems and structures which curtail Christian imagination. This fifth characteristic is, in many ways, a foil to the fourth. The Christian mind is accountable to, but not the unqualified servant of, the community of faith. For the Christian mind to be truly Christian, there must be room left to challenge systems and structures that would sustain distorted or incomplete accounts of the Christian community's imagined social existence together. Systems and structures which marginalize or otherwise silence voices seeking to reimagine the way of things through legitimate engagement with Scripture, tradition, and community, hinder transformative Christian discourse.

The Christian mind is not committed to the status quo. It does not believe that the way things are is the way things should be. Rather, it is because the Christian mind recognizes that everything is not as it should be that the status quo cannot remain forever. The systems and structures upholding that status quo by pressing out or demeaning voices that threaten to change the status quo's imagined social existence are products of a Christian mind with a diminished understanding of the sovereignty of God.

Jeremiah 7 is a paradigmatic text in this regard. Those who saw the temple as a sign of God's blessing presence despite the corruption of the nation refused to let go of its standard narrative. The status quo blinded those who should have been calling for reform. As the institutions of Israel became more and more corrupt, it became more and more clear that they were incapable of carrying forward a faithful testimony. It would not be up to the institutions to carry the faith of Israel forward, but to the people of Israel. God promises a New Covenant saying, "I will put my law within them, and I will write it on their hearts. And I will be their God, and they shall be my people. And no longer shall each one teach his neighbor and each his brother, saying, 'Know the Lord,' for they shall all know me, from the least of them to the greatest, declares the Lord. For I will forgive their iniquity, and I will remember their sin no more" (Jer 31:31-34).

Resisting systems and structures does not give individuals or groups license to use any means to accomplish a new end. Rather, the Christian mind recognizes that dethroning one regime in favor of another will only curtail Christian imagination in different ways and will only achieve the appearance of wisdom, transformation, and progress. Justice is not achieved by employing unjust means, nor is systemic oppression eliminated by oppressing a new group. In rejecting systems and structures that curtail Christian imagination, we must also resist the temptation to change for change's sake. As Johnson notes, "Christian allegiance is not to a single tradition but to the gospel, not to the task of reform for reform's sake, but to Christ."[22]

There must be a sober recognition that the human mind is incapable of fixing what is wrong in the world when disconnected from God. At the same time, the Christian mind is not justified in any action simply by connection with God. Instead, the Christian mind seeks to avoid repeating Moses's mistake when he attempted to deliver Israel in his own time and with his own strength (Exod 2:11-15). As impactful as the exodus narrative has been for those in need of deliverance, perhaps one of the most undervalued moments in the narrative occurs when Moses takes up the mantle of deliverer of his own accord and fails. A Christian mind sees the futility in acting apart from God.

Sixth, the Christian mind accepts the temporal, transient nature of people and institutions. Great, faithful leaders do not live forever and "golden ages" are a fleeting blessing.[23] The body of Christ will endure, but empires and institutions will run their course. The Christian mind does not simply resist systems and structures that hinder the community from conforming more fully to the image of Christ, it also resists the urge to sustain institutions or programs that God has used despite the fact that God is no longer using them. As Tozer is often quoted as saying, "If the Holy Spirit was withdrawn from the church today, 95 percent of what we do would go on and no one would know the difference." It is the goal of the Christian mind to commit to the 5 percent that is driven by the Spirit (and increase it!) rather than being content with the 95 percent that would continue apart from God. In this sense, at least, the Christian mind is unsentimental. Broken systems and structures are allowed to run their natural course without interventions designed to preserve them.

In part, this is a function of the Christian mind's deep historical awareness, which cultivates the understanding that the body of Christ has not always had the systems and structures of the modern-day church. Before there was the megachurch, there was the looser network of house churches. Before there was email, Facebook, or RightNow Media, Paul, Peter, James, and John wrote physical letters to convey theology and to influence congregations across a wide geography. The body of Christ is not beholden to any given situation or structure, however lamentable it may be to lose one. The Christian mind is less concerned with the preservation of a particular vehicle than it is committed to doing what it takes to ensure God's people sojourn faithfully.

Seventh, the Christian mind acknowledges the tensions involved in retaining Christian identity while participating in, yet remaining distinct from, the world. In *You Belong to Christ*, Tucker argues persuasively that Paul does not seek "to obliterate Jewish identity, or gentile identity for that matter."[24] Instead, Paul "understood social and cultural identities to be vital to the fulfillment of his mission as long as they did not contradict God's commands (e.g. immorality, idolatry, cultural boasting, or unscriptural patterns of thinking)."[25] It is not so much that we must be only Christian, but that our Christian identity cannot be compromised or superseded by other commitments.

Retaining Christian identity as primary without disallowing other social and cultural identities creates an ambiguous situation requiring deep, thoughtful engagement with the scriptures, the core doctrines of the church, the diverse theological traditions of church history, and the social and cultural commitments of particular moments in and across time. It also requires a rethinking of the nature of the theological process. Our understanding of God and what it means to be one of his people is forged in the crucible of our lived experience…at the intersection of text and life. God meets us as we struggle with the complexities of our existence helping us to understand ourselves as his children who exist in the world within unique social and cultural configurations.

By recognizing the tensions involved in retaining Christian identity while participating in and remaining distinct from the world, the Christian mind holds stubbornly to unity being slow to create or deepen fissures within the community of faith. The Christian mind also refuses to allow its thinking and discourse to be overdetermined by the frameworks, questions, or choices defined by the world. This refusal does not deny the importance of attending to contemporary questions or challenges. Rather, it is a refusal to be boxed in by a set of solutions or approaches limited by human capabilities and uniformed by the possibilities God provides.

Eighth, the Christian mind is, to borrow a term from Nassim Taleb, antifragile. In his book *Antifragile: Things that Gain from Disorder*, Taleb argues that there are certain things that benefit from stress. Unlike the fragile which shatters when pressure is applied, the antifragile may initially break down only to come back stronger.[26] For instance, when muscle is put under stress through resistance training, the tissues tear only to heal and come back stronger than they were before the stress was applied. Muscles, to a point, benefit from stress and strain as do bones and various other anatomical parts of the human body. In this sense, they may be thought of as antifragile.

The Christian mind, and the body of Christ more generally, are antifragile. It is not that the Christian mind is always right or immune from error. The Christian mind is often wrong. It has blind spots. It is willful, proud, and more rebellious than it should be. It can be unyielding and slow to conform to new ways of thought. It is often more defensive and risk averse than necessary. The Christian mind is not a perfect, fully sanctified mind. It is not antifragile because of some unique biological characteristic or collective genius. It is antifragile because when it is wrong…when its imperfections become evident...the Christian mind is refreshed, strengthened, and enlivened by the faithfulness of God whose lovingkindness is forever and whose compassion never fails. The Christian mind does not thrive in a pristine environment free of stressors and real-world challenges, but is strengthened and sharpened through trials (even trials that are self-inflicted).

As such, the Christian mind has nothing to fear from past errors, missed opportunities, change, scandal, or any other sort of mistake, challenge, or stressor. Individuals and communities exercising a Christian mind may be torn and broken down by certain people or events. Even in the midst of hardship the Christian mind can find the peace that surpasses all understanding, forgive those who commit inappropriate acts (physical or otherwise), show grace despite deep hurt or disagreement, lament the state of things, and, most of all, lean back on the sure rock of Christ knowing that hope is never lost. The Christian mind is antifragile because each new challenge and failure that reveals the weakness of the Christian mind only serves to point that same mind to the limitless strength, love, mercy, and loyalty of God. Our weakness reveals his strength (2 Cor. 12:1-9).

The Christian mind is antifragile because the God to whom the Christian mind is devoted has called those who believe to move from darkness to light by embracing truth (however difficult or inconvenient) not simply through affirmation and obedience, but through confession, repentance, forgiveness, and reconciliation. The Christian mind recognizes that our incompleteness reinforces key aspects of our imagined social existence. The church is always a community in process. The Christian mind recognizes that it will have shortcomings and blind spots. It recognizes the need for the diverse array of voices and perspectives within the body of Christ, and its dependence on the continued grace of the benevolent God it serves.

Conclusion

I am quite sure that there are other aspects of the Christian mind that I have not addressed here. Blamires, for instance, offers more in-depth treatment of six complementary "marks" of the Christian mind.[27] In setting out to offer a broad sketch of the Christian mind, I hope I have set the stage for the essays that follow. In essence, the Christian mind at the collective level offers a context in which Christians may discuss and discern what it means to imagine Christian social existence in the world. Individual Christian minds find a home within this collective context and commit to contributing to the discourse of the community of faith. Without the Christian mind, the community of faith surrenders itself (in whole or in part) to the imagined social existence of the world. In this imagined social existence politics, advocacy, power plays, quests for justice, and even civil discourse and discussion take on forms that, while possibly having the appearance of righteousness, are devoid of God.[28]

3 Christian Thought In A World Of Excess

Introduction

Whereas Orwell's dystopian vision was concerned with totalitarian regimes, Huxley described a situation in which people surrendered their desire (and ability) to think. As Postman writes,

> "…Huxley and Orwell did not prophesy the same thing…What Orwell feared were those who would ban books. What Huxley feared was that there would be no reason to ban a book, for there would be no one who wanted to read one. Orwell feared those who would deprive us of information. Huxley feared those who would give us so much that we would be reduced to passivity and egoism….In short, Orwell feared that what we hate will ruin us. Huxley feared that what we love will ruin us."[29]

While it is not clear that Orwell was wrong, it does seem that Huxley was on to something…we do enjoy our distractions and our distractions (at least some of them) are changing the way we interact with the world around us. Even if we aren't amusing ourselves to death at the moment, we are at a far greater risk of doing so when we have powerful, increasingly automated mechanisms for meeting our desires (some of which we don't even know we have).[30]

Such a situation contributes to the new consumer culture described by Cavanaugh:

> "Greed usually signifies an inordinate attachment to money and

things…But this view of greed does not really capture the spirit of our consumer economy. Most people are not overly attached to things, and most are not obsessed with hoarding riches….What really characterizes consumer culture is not attachment to things but detachment. People do not hoard money; they spend it. People do not cling to things; they discard them and buy other things."[31]

While Postman's critique of show business culture and the "trivialization of public information" is eerily accurate even today, there is more to be said. With his first edition published in 1985, Postman was not privy to much of what we know today about addictive behavior and neuroscience, which would seem to reinforce many of his concerns. Postman was also writing prior to the age of the helicopter parent and the "coddling of the American mind" which, as Jonathan Haidt and Greg Lukianoff argue, is having a detrimental impact on the way the younger generation thinks.[32]

Postman reminds us that "spiritual devastation is more likely to come from an enemy with a smiling face."[33] Whatever else may be said, it is within this new world, a world of instant gratification via, among other things, the internet, that the Christian mind is currently being forged. We can either busy ourselves by looking at pictures of friends on Instagram, searching for the best deal on Amazon.com, or watching the Kylie Jenner "To Our Daughter" video (the #1 video of 2018 with over 80 million views…and counting), or we can take seriously our calling from darkness to light by making sharp the Christian mind. We certainly have agency and responsibility even in the digital age, yet we also have new obstacles to overcome and those obstacles are not always obvious. Like a frog being boiled in a pot, we may not recognize that the heat is rising to dangerous levels until it is too late.

This essay will address three key obstacles: (1) misdirected desires and the systems that support them, (2) contentment (or lack thereof), and (3) the cultivation of dispositions that detract from Christian thought. These three dangers are particularly problematic because they are less noticeable than problems like the oft-cited issue of "Biblical literacy."[34] None of the dangers discussed are inevitable, but they are interconnected. Christian thought and practice can counteract these dangers through discipleship in which Christ becomes so compelling that looking away to distractions becomes unthinkable or at least less and less appealing.

To develop such thought and practice, however, we must recognize that we are not always dealing with sins that can be confronted head on. Not all problems can be solved by pointing to a particular Bible verse and demanding obedience to it. Instead, we will need to reconsider what it means to make disciples in a context where our ability to fulfill virtually every fleeting desire may well keep us from cultivating the deeper longings of our heart. We need to be diligent in creating a community where disciples may be formed for whom a deepening knowledge of God is paramount. Perhaps most importantly, we must reckon with the depth of our own sin by committing to reorient our desires and ambitions so as to seek the good of God's people.

Obstacle 1: Misdirected Desires and the Systems that Support Them

Addiction studies demonstrate "a glut of evidence that natural rewards are capable of inducing plasticity in addiction-related circuitry."[35] Translation: our brains like rewards of all sorts and can become addicted to surfing the internet, internet gaming, and a host of other activities in a way similar to becoming addicted to heroin, cocaine, or alcohol. While I do not wish to call for an internet temperance movement, Christians must give some thought to the manner in which seemingly innocuous activities like searching for content on Google, waiting for "likes" on a Facebook post, or refreshing a screen to see if the counter on your blog has increased, can begin to dominate our thinking. We have embedded ourselves into a new sort of technological-enhanced system, which is shaping the way we act and interact in a variety of ways.

Systems matter. In *Atomic Habits,* James Clear calls attention to the power of system-forming habits noting, "You do not rise to the level of your goals. You fall to the level of your systems."[36] The idea is quite simple: goals matter far less than we might assume because the systems of which we are a part have a powerful impact on the way we think and act. More significantly such systems influence our core identity. Clear emphasizes the central importance of identity change:

> "The more deeply a thought or action is tied to your identity, the more difficult it is to change. It can feel comfortable to believe what your culture believes (group identity) or to do what upholds your self-image (personal identity), even if it's wrong. The biggest barrier to positive change at any level—individual, team, society—is identity conflict. Good habits can make rational sense, but if they conflict with your identity, you will fail to put them into action."[37]

The systems we inhabit participate in shaping our identity. They condition (in helpful and unhelpful ways) our underlying beliefs about God, ourselves, and the world around us. They have the ability to create and reinforce desires …misdirected or otherwise.

The systems we currently inhabit are different than those of previous generations and have different forming effects, but it is not as though we have only recently entered an era of systems. Surely internet addiction was not available before the rise of the World Wide Web. Perhaps it was not even available prior to the broad availability of higher-speed internet and the onset of smartphones. Yet the systems of a bygone, "analog" era formed our identity and habits just the same. Perhaps some of these dynamics did not rise to the level of addiction, but blaming the internet for what is a deeper human tendency seems as odd as blaming a baseball for intentionally hitting a batter (when it is clearly the pitcher's fault). Solving the internet problem won't eliminate the issue of formative systems.

That past generations struggled with the systems of which they were a part is evident in the writings of past Christian figures. Augustine, for instance, recognized the ease with which we become consumed with the praise of others, particularly within certain "offices" (which I take to be loosely analogous to a system) The "well done" becomes the all-consuming reward toward which we are compelled to strive:

"Because now certain offices of human society make it necessary to be loved and feared of men, the adversary of our true blessedness lays hard at us, everywhere spreading his snares of 'well-done, well-done;' that greedily catching at them, we may be taken unawares, and sever our joy from Thy truth, and set it in the deceivingness of man; and be pleased at being loved and feared, not for Thy sake, but in Thy stead…"[38]

We cannot deny our responsibility to reflect on our systems, consider our desires, and to discipline ourselves so as to build systems and structures that conform us more closely to the image of Christ.

Recognizing the role of systems is one thing, but understand the mechanisms of addiction are quite another. Whereas systems like those of Augustine's offices surely exerted a degree of pressure that conditioned the behaviors of those who occupied them, our current technological systems have upped the ante. The technology systems with which we interact do more than exert pressure…they compete heavily with the "real world" for mind space to such an extent that "a form of techno-quicksand sucks us in and reduces our satisfaction at work and at home, puts us at mortal risk on the roads, and invades our most intimate moments to weave an unhealthy web of compulsion and dependency"[39]

Understanding the mechanisms of addiction begins to become crucial to understanding how we might faithfully navigate the digital age in which we live. As Love notes, "There is a key element found throughout all internet-related experiences: The ability to maintain or heighten arousal with the click of a mouse or swipe of a finger."[40] The systems of which we are a part…those that make life easier and constitute the almost default way in which we interact with the world…shape in us beliefs and desires that are continually refreshed and reinforced by a quest for the new and novel.

Novelty plays a significant role in "repeatedly reinforcing the reward, motivation and memory circuitry" which "are all part of the diseases of addiction" because "it activates the brain's reward system."[41] Love emphasizes that, "…the act of seeking (which would include surfing) triggers the reward system. So do stimuli that violate expectations (positive or negative), which is often found in today's videogames [*sic*] and internet pornography."[42] Once we believe that what we have is not as good as what we could get, we become embedded within a system in which we privilege the object of our desires…even to our detriment.

Acting against our best interests (engaging in behavior resulting in negative consequences) isn't necessarily indicative of "addiction." Identifying the threshold for what constitutes addiction is challenging. For example, normally described as excessive participation in the internet resulting in negative consequences, internet addiction and associated disorders are not without ambiguity. People can make decisions that have negative consequences for a host of reasons unrelated to addiction.

In their review of internet addiction literature, Van Rooij and Prause rightly note the challenges associated with clearly distinguishing "negative consequences" from "non-optimal decision-making."[43] The main challenge is that both negative consequences, which would be understood as outcomes, and non-optimal decisions, which would be understood as voluntary actions, look eerily similar:

> "The negative consequences criterion has strong face validity, as it is difficult to imagine someone voluntarily choosing to suffer negative consequences. Mental illness, such as substance addiction, is often inferred from behavior tenacity in the face of these negative consequences. However, research on decision-making consistently demonstrates circumstances under which healthy people engage in non-optimal, and often ultimately detrimental, behaviors."[44]

The goal of this discussion is not to identify the line between negative outcomes derived from addiction and those derived from non-optimal decision making, nor is it to suggest that addiction is not a real, neurological phenomenon for which many people need medical or psychological interventions. Instead, the goals are to (a) highlight the very real dangers we face as we exist within systems, particularly the increasingly ever-present digital systems, that form and shape our underlying identities and (b) call each of us to seriously evaluate how evaluating our systems and the decision-making strategies we employ within them might lessen the "negative consequences" we experience.

There are a variety of non-optimal choice types available in any given scenario. We have a variety of different biases that can skew our perception of reality. As Chip and Dan Heath note, "Our normal habit in life is to develop a quick belief about a situation and then seek out information that bolsters our belief."[45] Our decision making is seldom optimal because the process in which we engage to come to a decision seldom involves "…exploring alternative points of view, recognizing uncertainty, searching for evidence that contradicts their [our] belief…"[46]

Moreover, we often make non-optimal decisions because we are fooled by a phenomenon that Gilbert and Wilson call "miswanting." Miswanting is a particular fallacy of logic whereby we mistake the projected significance of a given decision to our future well-being and end up making poor choices. Saying what we want, in Gilbert and Wilson's analysis, tends to be "about those things that we believe will influence our sense of well-being, satisfaction, happiness, and contentment."[47] In our zeal to get what we want we "tend to imagine a particular event while making little provision for the possibility that the particular event they are imagining may not necessarily be the particular event they will be experiencing."[48]

Gilbert and Wilson suggest two primary factors contributing to our "naïve analysis of happiness." The first is our tendency to "misconstrue events, misunderstand ourselves, misinterpret our feelings."[49] We "miswant," in part, because we have a fundamental misunderstanding of who we are (identity), what we feel, and how we relate to our surroundings. The second is that "liking does not *follow* from getting so much as it *accommodates* it."[50] In other words, we have a vested interest in being happy and tend to turn as many frowns upside down as possible. Even if the decisions we make lead us into "non-optimal" situations we don't necessarily care to admit it.

Addiction, non-optimal decision-making, and "miswanting" all point to a similar problem...we don't always know what we want even when we really think we do. It isn't just a matter of rebellion, but of delusion.[51] Chemical dependencies and physiological mechanisms aside, our identities are forged within the systems of a fallen world. Unless we are diligent in the development of our theological social imaginaries, we will always be at a higher risk of being more formed by the world than by the God who created it.

The Christian tradition goes further noting that it is not simply that we have misdirected desires (we do not simply miswant), but that those misdirected desires bring bondage. We lose ourselves to our desires. Commenting on Augustine's theology of sin, Thistleton identifies two key themes: "the primacy of God's grace, and an understanding of sin as misdirected desire that brings bondage and self-destructive consequences."[52] Our misdirected desire is an extension of our misrecognition of our own identity in Christ. We are no longer a broken people incapable of wisely navigating the world. We are now a broken people united in Christ who, through the power of the Holy Spirit, have the opportunity to live as those called from darkness to light.

God has created us not only to know or understand, but to enjoy. As limited creatures we are not self-sufficient, nor are we complete in and of ourselves. We need. As we feel those needs, we cultivate desires...yet even appropriate desires can be misdirected. As we search for something to fill the voids in our souls, our bodies, and our relationships, we must understand deeply the degree to which our broken relationship with God has damaged our capacity to desire rightly, yet we must also understand how our renewed relationship with God offers us the capacity to re-direct our desires as we embed ourselves within a system...a community...committed to living in light of God and what he has done for us.

Problem 2: Contentment (or Lack Thereof)

In the song "7 Rings," Ariana Grande proclaims "Whoever said money can't solve your problems must not have had enough money to solve 'em."[53]

Though we might, as Christians, disagree with the lyric, our objections fall flat when not reinforced by a life characterized by contentment. There is only so much that our affirmation of theology and doctrine can convey because intellectual assent does not constitute a fully-formed Christian witness. The body of Christ cannot go on opposing the philosophies of the world in principle while living them out in practice. It is, as D.L. Moody once said, "The preaching that this world needs most is the sermons in shoes that are walking with Jesus Christ."[54]

My own early (and ultimately immature) theological reflections, were largely driven by a deep dissatisfaction with life and the way it seemed to be going. I had considered writing a book entitled *Embracing Mediocrity* that would mourn my lackluster career, lament my poor decisions, bemoan my wasted opportunities, and lay out the coping mechanisms I would seek to use as I plodded slowly toward retirement (and death). I'm sure it would have been quite a page turner. I'm equally sure that it would have been an unfaithful rendering of God and the work He was seeking to do in my life.

At that point and throughout much of my life, professional contentment has escaped me. My ambition, desire to have more than I've been given, and individualistic understanding of the Christian life combined to produce a deeply rooted sense of dissatisfaction. Nothing less than getting everything I wanted (and more) would have been enough to satisfy me. As Ricky Bobby said, "If you ain't first, you're last."[55] What I had was never as good as what I could have gotten. I gave myself over to a vicious cycle in which the more I got, the more I wanted.

That cycle is not unique to me. In his book entitled *The Naked Consumer*, Larson highlights the industrial impulse to create a need for more. Note his observations concerning the strategies of automakers in the 1920's: "…General Motors began making annual changes in body styles, a practice that came to be known as 'planned obsolescence.' The stated mission of GM's research division was 'the organized creation of dissatisfaction.'"[56] GM was turning discontentment into a science and exploiting what seems to be a quite pernicious temptation to "keep up with the Joneses." It would seem that we have an uphill battle if we are to avoid engaging in an obsessive quest to capture the "next big thing."[57]

Our goal should not be to change our situation in order to be content, but to find contentment in every situation. In speaking of his own contentment in Philippians 4, Paul notes that he has learned to be content in every situation…whether "facing plenty and hunger, abundance and need" (Phil 4:12). Paul's situation is immaterial to his contentment because he finds sufficiency not in his own capacities or in his circumstances, but through the One who strengthens him (4:13).

The revelation in Paul's statement in Philippians is that contentment is not situational…one's contentment is not linked to the vicissitudes of life. Instead, contentment is learned as we acknowledge our insufficiency and Christ's full sufficiency. It is a question of embracing who God requires us to be. Who we are is not tied up with our material life, but with being a faithful presence regardless of our individual or collective circumstances. As Moltmann rightly notes, "Temptation then consists not so much in the titanic desire to be as God, but in weakness, timidity, weariness, not wanting to be what God requires of us."[58]

Considering temptation from this perspective, puts Paul's learned contentment into new perspective. As noted above, contentment problems are often (rightly) framed in terms of some sense of deficit…we do not have all we need (or want). The somewhat surprising perspective that Paul offers is that he has learned to be content with "plenty" and in "abundance." It would seem that Paul has broken through to the governing dynamics of any situation in which he finds himself…he is to represent Christ regardless of his circumstances. As such, he can neither be obsessed with what he lacks, nor seduced by what he has. Paul has learned to "be what God requires" of him whether he has more than he needs or less than he wants.

The point here is that discontentment with our lot in life is not due to our circumstances but to our unwillingness to learn contentment. We refuse to learn what it means to be "what God requires" and to locate our life in Christ and His body. If this sort of learned contentment applies across all of our situations, we must quickly realize that the sort of contentment Paul speaks of has everything to do with being settled in one's own in-Christ identity.

If discontentment is not only associated with "hunger" and "need," but also with "plenty" and "abundance," we must reckon not only with the sort of discontent that comes through want, but also with the pseudo-contentment that fears loss. In a world of excess, we see the impulse to be less-than satisfied with meager circumstances and to be too satisfied with prosperity. The former breeds discontentment, in part, through comparison. When others are living what we perceive to be a sufficiently "better life," we quickly find ourselves less satisfied with our own circumstances.

The latter produces pseudo-contentment as we determine not to risk what we have. It is a pseudo-contentment because it is not grounded in Christ, but in what Christ has given. Prosperity has a way of cultivating a peculiar sort of Stockholm syndrome in which we identify with our material captors. Chittister's criticism of her generation's lackluster efforts to address "great causes" offers a helpful example of this latter sort of pseudo-contentment. The inability (or unwillingness) to address "great causes" is characterized by "…trading commitment for conformity, by worshiping at the shrine of professionalism rather than prophetism, by keeping the peace instead of raising a prophet's alarm and by guarding ourselves against death by choosing to die in place—clean, safe and proper."[59]

Understood as an ongoing recognition of Christ's sufficiency and of cultivating a desire to "be what God requires of us," contentment calls on us to imagine our social existence through a decidedly theological framework in which we are drawn into the life of the Triune God through faith in Christ. We do not exist as beings resigned to the current state of things (no matter how comfortable or uncomfortable they may be for us). Rather, we exist as a people assured that the world will not remain as it is, but will succumb to the

"…kingdom of God, which will redeem everything and put all things to rights, the kingdom which will come 'on earth as it is in heaven.'"[60]

Contentment cannot be found in possessions or prosperity. It can only be found in Christ. To learn such contentment, however, requires us to learn, as Paul did, to be content "in whatever situation" (4:11). Such learning is hard earned…it is not knowledge abstracted from experience, but born in the crucible and comfort of the Christian experience. Learning from experience requires more than just surviving or enjoying the experience. It requires that certain dispositions and "patterns of movement" be developed so that we exist within our varied experiences as a faithful presence content in Christ.

Problem 3: Dispositions that Hinder Christian Thought

Perhaps the best analogy for what Pierre Bourdieu had in mind when he used the term *habitus* is the sort of coordination that one develops through dance.[61] Movements are under control, fitted within a particular style and tradition, yet gracefully and naturally rendered in a unique combination of seemingly effortless movements. Developing the ability to perform these movements requires immense amounts of time, thought, and repetition. It requires an understanding of each individual movement, how multiple movements fit together, and what the movements are capable of communicating. More than that, it requires dancers to sustain a certain mental, emotional, and physical state so that they are capable of performing the movements that they have worked so hard to learn and that have become so natural.

Christians aren't required to pirouette (thankfully), but we do live out our faith through the development of specific dispositions and disciplines that allow us to exhibit a natural, graceful way of being in the world. As we gain coordination and understand how to move faithfully within our varied experiences, we also develop within us a particular way of thinking about the world around us. We learn to offer embodied testimony on terms fitted to the context in which we find ourselves, yet not determined by that context. We often offer counter-testimony to rebut or expand on the underlying social imaginaries of a world that does not know God.

As the church begins to span generations in which social, cultural, political, and economic landscapes are changing, it may feel like Christianity is becoming unmoored from biblical authority and the traditions of the church (and that may be true in certain cases). Locating the whole of the problem with generational or cultural shifts that no longer align with a particular notion of "biblical values" or "Christian ethics," however, obscures the fact that there has never been a golden age of Christianity to which we, particularly in American evangelicalism, may harken back. No such time seems to have ever actually existed.

Instead, we have largely suffered from "built-in barriers to productive thinking."[62] Mark Noll describes several such barriers in *Jesus Christ and the Life of the Mind*:

> "These barriers include an immediatism that insists on action, decision, and even perfection *right now*; a populism that confuses winning supporters with mastering actually existing situations; and an antitraditionalism that privileges current judgments on biblical, theological, and ethical issues (however hastily formed) over insight from the past (however hard won and carefully stated)...we evangelicals are susceptible to a nearly gnostic dualism that rushes to spiritualize all manner of corporeal, terrestrial, physical, and material realities...We also prefer to put our money into programs offering immediate relief, whether evangelistic or humanitarian, instead of into institutions promoting intellectual development over the long term."[63]

Christian thought has, to some extent, been made captive to present circumstances and suffers from a narrowed vision (not a wrong vision, but a narrowed vision) of what it means to render God faithfully to the world. This narrowed vision creates a context in which we often fall prey to confirmation bias. All the evidence (at least the evidence we are willing to evaluate) leads us to confirm our pre-existing beliefs and practices.

Our concerns that specific "watershed" issues will, if not resolved correctly, fracture the church and cause us to fall into a state of abject moral decay, are quite often overstated and under-thought. Perhaps worse, topics such as gender roles in the church and whether or not women should hold the office of elder have, in certain instances, diminished the dignity of women and given men an excuse to exercise a perverted authority within the body of Christ. The vehemence with which the church has opposed divorce has not been matched by a commitment to holding men and women accountable for their non-sexual activity in marriage (e.g. emotional and verbal abuse). Our obsession with preserving conservative values and other *non-theological* identity markers has not always been matched with the cultivation of a strong theological, Christian identity in the church that is separate from the systems and structures of the world around us.[64]

All of these topics (and a host of others) have passed through my mind at various points in my career. While I still find myself pondering them on occasion, I view them more as distractions than as productive conversation starters. Why is that? In part, it is rooted in my general agreement with Noll's analysis. Christian thought has too often succumbed to immediacy and an ahistorical, spiritualized pragmatism that keeps us less connected and less concerned with passing on a faithful, thoughtful legacy. Addressing specific topics feels like we are handing a band-aid to someone with a severed limb.

We may well be right to feel a sense of urgency to share the gospel with the world or to right the social and individual wrongs we see before us. We are wrong, however, to think that the patient acts of prayer and fasting, the emotive cry of lamentation, or the slow, thoughtful engagement of the scriptures and theology are not appropriate expressions of such urgency. Once we adopt a disposition in which those who pray engage in an empty ritual or those who lament in a form of self-centered whining or those who think deeply are isolating themselves within some sort of ivory tower, we can be sure that we have made God a figure head instead of a ruler.

Our concern with the present and willingness to skewer internal and external opposition over disagreements suggests that we represent a God who desires to overpower rather than overwhelm. The difference is slight, but significant. The former cultivates arrogance as we cling with white-knuckles to "the truth of God's word" abstracted from the challenges and complexities for which God's word is uniquely qualified to deal. The latter cultivates a humble strength through which God's people become capable of embracing a world within which they move and act, but to which they are not beholden.

Our disposition should not reflect the adoption of an "I'm ok, your ok" sort of philosophy, nor should it reflect a resignation to despair over the ways in which the world is not as it should be. The former downplays the severity of sin while the latter gives sin too much power. We are victors *in Christ*. It is the victory that speaks to our strength…our steely resolve to live with God in a world that does not acknowledge Him. It is the "in Christ" that cultivates humility. We are not, in and of ourselves, victors. We did not achieve victory in our own strength. We were made victors through faith in Christ who defeated sin and death (1 Cor 15:50-57). We are not strong because we have confidence in ourselves and our own abilities. Instead, we find strength in our weakness knowing that we are united with Christ. We are humble not because we discount our God-given abilities. We are humble because we know that even our strongest attributes were given by God for His use and in His wisdom.

When our disposition is one of humble strength, we recognize that the problems of the world are ours to navigate faithfully…not to solve. Christians will leave the world broken, perhaps more broken despite our faithful efforts to live out the kingdom of God within it. We do not faithfully convey God to the world by fixing the world. We convey Him to the world by continuing to be faithful as we confront a world so broken only God can fix it.

Conclusion

In a world of excess, Christian thought is challenged by more than greed. Christian thought is also under threat from the waves of information that threaten to drown Christian thought with sheer volume. It is also under threat from the systems and structures that drive us to remain anxious in the moment…to need immediate responses and easy answers. Most of all, however, Christian thought is under threat in an age of excess because the church has not been able to cultivate a Christian mind sufficient to shape disciples who understand what it means to be content in all circumstances…to be what God requires them to be regardless of the situation in which they find themselves.

4 Cultivating A Christian Mind

Introduction

The Christian mind is not solely contained within a single individual's head, but is comprised of the broader discourse environment in which the body of Christ operates within the world. Changing societies is a complex matter requiring fundamental shifts in the underlying conceptions of morality. Such conceptions go "beyond some proposed schedule of norms that ought to govern our mutual relations and/or political life…the image of order carries a definition not only of what is right, but of the context in which it makes sense to strive for and hope to realize the right (at least partially)."[65]

Taylor describes the social imaginary as existing between explicit doctrines and embodied practices. The social imaginary is "nourished in embodied *habitus*" and "given expression on the symbolic level."[66] That these three areas of doctrine, practice, and symbol, intersect and influence one another suggests that there could be a number of potential avenues for change, as well as a number of complex obstacles preventing it.

Cultivating a Christian mind calls for a renovation of the Christian social imaginary, as well as an evaluation of embodied practices within the context of established Christian doctrine and an ongoing interaction with the scriptures. Borrowing Castoriadis's notion of autonomous societies, the Christian community is uniquely capable of critically reflecting on its social imaginaries and the institutions that arise from them.⁶⁷ While it might appear that Christian community is more rigid due to its doctrinal commitments, the opposite is actually the case. The community's ongoing interaction with the scriptures continually destabilizes (or should destabilize) settled notions related to underlying social imaginaries and embedded practices. Deep engagement with the scriptures is essential, but not generally sufficient, to the cultivation of a Christian mind,.

Living out a social imaginary different from that of the surrounding culture requires not only courage and boldness, but a creative mind and a willingness to accept loss on some level. Resisting the urge to conform to the ways of the world is not a trivial matter, nor is recognizing the adoption of a social imaginary that is less-than Christian. Thus, cultivating a Christian mind will likely require more than resolve, tenacity, and will power. The Christian mind is developed through a more elegant, intentional process that involves the design of a system for building habits aligned with doctrine and rooted within a Christian social imaginary. Such a system is necessary because the "present climate of opinion" both within the church and without creates pressures that hinder Christian discourse and thought.

"The Present Climate of Opinion"

When he wrote *The Christian Mind* in 1963, Harry Blamires does not paint an overly optimistic picture for the future of Christian thought. He calls the church to develop a Christian mind while recognizing the particular challenges of "the present climate of opinion" which "makes it impossible to avoid taking these steps without opening oneself to charges of 'bigotry,' 'dogmatism,' 'doctrinaire intolerance,' and without incurring that most crushing of all contemporary smears—that one is being 'holier-than-thou.'"⁶⁸ While the context in which the church and its members seek to develop a Christian mind today have changed, one would be hard-pressed to suggest that our current "climate of opinion" is more conducive to the cultivation of a Christian mind than it was in Blamires' day.

Blamires' insight concerning the challenge of the "climate of opinion" is an important one that finds support in other fields. For instance, in their chapter entitled "Intimidation and Violence," Lukianoff and Haidt examine the polarization of discourse and the impact it has on thought and expression particularly on college campuses. Recounting several instances similar to the "Milo riot" at UC Berkley, Lukianoff and Haidt describe the challenges associated with the "pick a side" mentality that sees speech as violence.

In essence, the 'holier-than-thou' label no longer applies to Christians alone, but to any group or individual speaking (or thinking) in ways that have "a negative impact on vulnerable members of the community."[69] Lukianoff and Haidt suggest that this situation is detrimental to discourse and, thus, thought:

> "The Columbia University linguist John McWhorter describes how the term 'white supremacist' is now used in an 'utterly athletic, recreational" way, as a 'battering ram' to attack anyone who departs from the party line…But if some students now think it's OK to punch a fascist or white supremacist, and if anyone who disagrees with them can be labeled a fascist or white supremacist, well, you can see how this rhetorical move might make people hesitant to voice dissenting views on campus."[70]

This dynamic is not limited to college students, but is evident among faculty members as well: "Professors try to round up hundreds of other professors to condemn a fellow professor or to demand that an academic article be retracted (rather than simply rebutting it)."[71] While Lukianoff and Haidt offer examples from secular colleges, it would seem that such dynamics could easily be heightened within a confessional context where certain arenas of inquiry are considered taboo.[72]

Beyond the dynamics associated with the "coddling" that Lukianoff and Haidt note, Caplan offers a sustained critique of education as a system. In *The Case against Education: Why the Education System is a Waste of Time and Money*, Caplan identifies signaling as the primary problem with the current education system, particularly the signaling of conformity. Essentially, "signaling" is associated with the inferences drawn from one's educational history. For example, Caplan notes, "Even if what a student learned in school is utterly useless, employers will happily pay extra if their scholastic achievements provides information about their productivity...Your educational record reveals much about your ability and character."[73] Education signals conformity not "in some abstract sense," but to a more specific conception of a "model worker" that involves education. Caplan observes,

> "In our society, educational achievement is a social expectation. Model workers are supposed to pursue and obtain traditional credentials: a high school diploma for virtually any job, a bachelor's degree for a good job. If you violate these expectations, you're moderately nonconformist. If you defy these expectations, you're extremely nonconformist. When you lack credentials, the best back-up signal of conformity isn't to denounce credentialism, but to humbly hold your tongue."[74]

To the extent that Caplan's argument concerning signaling is correct, it also makes those hiring complicit in the overarching system. The criteria, for instance, of evaluating a candidate for a position within a theological institution, ministry, or church may well eliminate viable candidates simply on the basis of credentials (or lack thereof) by assuming the presence of characteristics that may not actually be present or will not be carried over from one context (e.g. academic performance) to another (e.g. a leadership position or tenured faculty role). Regardless, it would appear that there is some conception of the "model worker" to which those with any level of training will need to conform.

Support for Blamires' view concerning the "climate of opinion" is also found outside of the literature concerned with education. In their work on social identity theory, for instance, Klein, Spears, and Reicher note the significance of powerful "out-group" influence on the expression of "in-group" identity. Basically, external factors can and do condition the manner in which we express our own identities. As Klein, Spears, and Reicher note, "Group behavior is a matter of the practical ability to act as well as the motivational and/or cognitive instigation to act."[75] In other words, identity performance, or "the purposeful expression (or suppression) of behaviors relevant to those norms conventionally associated with salient social identity," is not simply a matter of desire or motivation, but of actual ability to work out that identity in practical ways.[76]

If, as Blamires suggests, the "present climate of opinion" involves hostility toward genuine Christian thought…thought that begins with and refuses to decouple itself from a theological social imaginary…a Christian mind may become more and more difficult to sustain. Those seeking to develop a Christian mind must reckon with the challenges of doing so not only in the world, but in the church where dynamics such as those described by Lukianoff and Haidt can take root rather quickly. While labeling someone as a "white supremacist" may be less prominent in evangelical circles, the dreaded labels of "liberal," "postmodern," or "democrat" on the one hand and of "conservative," "modernist," or "republican" on the other have a similar effect…they divide, polarize, and, to a large extent, misrepresent.

As we consider what it means, then, to cultivate a Christian mind, we must reckon with the (false) notion that the Christian mind is defined by any given group or sect within Christendom. Despite the rather adamant claims of certain voices within evangelicalism, there is room for difference of opinion and a need to wrestle with the various positions of the church afresh in light of new challenges, new intellectual developments, and new voices. That is not to say that the consensus regarding the churches core doctrines should be up for grabs with any new generation. Rather, it is a recognition that the manner in which we understand truth is not the same as the truth itself, but is an approximation of the truth derived from a perspective embedded within a social imaginary or way of framing our everyday beliefs and practices.

We converse and question not to change enduring truth, but to reorient our perception of it and the manner in which we put such truth into practice. Vanhoozer calls this sort of questioning the "negative task" of theology by which we "critically reflect on the way in which the church embodies the prevailing social imaginaries of the day rather than the biblical imaginary—the true story of what the Triune God is doing in the world."[77] By submitting our common labels and categories to scrutiny in light of Scripture and doctrine, we may well find that what we thought were separate, polar opposite groupings have more in common than we might initially have assumed. After all, the Pharisees, Sadducees, and Scribes could be differentiated, yet they seemed to share a common propensity for anti-Jesus sentiment and false teaching.

While "conservative" and "liberal" are labels that are often used to categorize specific, opposing groups within Christian circles, a more fruitful categorization might be between those who default to specific cultural values (whether conservative or liberal) and those who scrutinize those values by privileging God's word and the doctrines of the church. It is just as easy to think less-than theologically while elevating conservative values to a place of prominence as it is while elevating liberal ones. Even basic theological commitments shared among those of a specific group are not necessarily sufficient to guard against the adoption of less-than theological patterns of thought. Such is one of the key problems when seeking to cultivate a Christian mind: we don't have categories sufficient to identify the relevant features constitutive of Christian thought…nor do we seem to feel any need to develop them.

Affirmation of core doctrine and theology is certainly a mark of inclusion within the community of faith; however, as Chester and Timmis note, "The theology that matters is not the theology we profess but the theology we practice."[78] As such, affirmation of theological positions is no guarantee of Christian thought, which must be made manifest within concrete situations and reflected in the social dynamics and structures of the the community.[79] Professing right doctrine is a necessary, but insufficient criteria for identifying the boundaries of the community of faith. There must also be a willingness to continually rethink and revise our individual and collective behaviors…the way we organize ourselves and interact with the world…if we are to show ourselves to be practitioners of "religion that is pure and undefiled" (James 1:27).

Reframing the Way We View the World

In order to cultivate a Christian mind, as well as navigating the challenges of the "present climate of opinion," the church will need to learn to reframe the way in which it sees and engages the world. The concept of reframing has been applied in a number of different disciplines from counseling to organizational leadership. Essentially, it involves a shift of mind and a reorientation of the mental scaffolding that structures the way in which we view the world: "Framing involves matching mental maps to circumstances. Reframing requires another skill—the ability to break frames."[80]

In some respects, the description of reframing as "the ability to break frames" reflects something akin to the mental shifts that Christians make when they proclaim the resurrection of Jesus Christ. O'Donovan points to this sort of shift in his discussion of Christian ethics noting,

> "…we cannot admit the suggestion that Christian ethics should pick its way between the two poles of law and licence [*sic*] in search of middle ground. Such an approach could end up by being only what it was from the start, an oscillation between two sub-Christian forms of life. A consistent Christianity must take a different path altogether, the path of an integrally evangelical ethics which rejoices the heart and gives light to the eyes because it springs from God's gift to mankind in Jesus Christ."[81]

Getting caught within a particular framework can blind us to viable alternatives that lie outside of our current field of vision. While there are numerous ways to go about reframing the world, four seem most pertinent for a people seeking to glorify and enjoy God in the midst of a world that is not as it should be: (1) engaging difference, (2) asking different questions, (3) considering systems, and (4) developing into expert Christians.[82]

<u>Engaging Difference</u>

One way in which we can put ourselves in a position to reframe the way we think is by encountering perspectives that are not our own…we must engage what is other. There is a wealth of literature demonstrating the value of certain types of diversity in certain types of situations. Page's work on diversity, for instance, highlights the importance of diversity in problem solving and predictive modeling.[83] Burt offers a similar insight from the perspective of social capital theory when he speaks of breaking out of "more homogeneous" ways of "thinking and behaving." He suggests, "…people who live in the intersection of social worlds are at higher risk of having good ideas."[84] Positioning oneself and one's community so as to benefit from the diverse perspectives of other groups brings with it the opportunity to reframe more effectively because "When minority voices are heard, well-functioning groups are likely to be jolted out of their routines…"[85]

While it may seem counter-intuitive to suggest that encountering the "other" is significant for the development of a Christian mind, it should be noted that interacting with diverse perspectives does not require the adoption of those perspectives. It is not a question of embracing some sort of relative notion of truth and reality whereby the Christian community gives away its convictions. Rather, it is a recognition that the perspectives of others are a source of endless potential. This point is similar to the insight offered by Taleb concerning Umberto Eco's library: "Read books are far less valuable than unread ones. The library should contain as much of what you do not know as your financial means, mortgage rates, and the currently tight real-estate market allow you to put there."[86]

Perhaps one of the most astute treatments of discourse with difference is found in John Stuart Mill's *On Liberty*. Mill argues for the allowance of differing opinions regardless of their apparent truthfulness or validity. He rightly notes that the suppression of difference is enacted by those who "are not infallible."[87] After all, a suppressed opinion may end up being true. Though it is certainly the case that the scriptures are infallible, the same cannot be said for those who interpret them.

To claim that we have so mastered God's word that we need no outside opinion from others is to forget that as we engage the scriptures, we encounter the Other who is God. Our convictions are both necessary and provisional to the extent that we are always hindered by our own incompleteness and subject to the living and active word of God that is never fully contained by any individual understanding or by the understanding of any given community within time. As Rush notes, "The horizons from which doctrines are understood, interpreted, and applied, change from generation to generation, from culture to culture, from context to context...past doctrinal formulation functions to provoke and ultimately change limited human horizons of expectation."[88] He also notes the significance of difference, or alterity, to experiencing God as other: "...God's alterity is immediately experienced mediately through the alterity of past horizons and the alterity of revelation taking place within present experience and the diverse horizons of contemporary reception."[89] At the risk of overstating the case, my suspicion is that an overzealous impulse to suppress the difference of *others* by closing down discussion cultivates a disposition less-than-sensitive to the transformative power of God...the ultimate *Other*.

Mill is not simply concerned that in suppressing difference we run the risk of missing the truth. He also recognizes the inherent weakness of an unchallenged, unreflective opinion noting, "He who knows only his own side of the case, knows little of that."[90] Again, the point is not to suggest that when challenged, one should simply change one's point of view. Rather, the point is that our opinions are forged in the fires of debate and disagreement. We come to hold our views with greater surety and confidence as we allow our perspectives to be tested in the crucible of conversation.

The final concern Mill expresses is that often truth is to be found in the intersection of conflicting views. The Christian mind need not fear the idea of being wrong, but the idea that the truth will be hindered because we are too afraid to test our understandings. Klein's demonstration that contradiction can produce insight would seem to align with Mill's view. Klein suggests, "Contradiction insights send us on the road to a better story. They signal that there's something seriously wrong with the story we're currently telling ourselves."[91]

Asking Different Questions

In *Simple Habits for Complex Times*, Berger and Johnston note, "The questions you ask will tell you a lot about the way you're seeing the world at that moment in time."[92] They go on to suggest, "Asking different questions is about shifting the mindset, and it is a reciprocal move: your questions can shift your mindset and your mindset can shift your questions."[93] In part, our actions and decisions are a reflection of the questions we ask ourselves. Whether those questions are explicit or implicit is of less consequence than the fact that we ask them. When explicit, questions will be rather simple to identify. When implicit, it will require us to reverse engineer the questions we are asking about the world that lead us to a particular behavior, decision, or perspective.

Perhaps the best place to begin the process of asking different questions is to identify the current set of questions we ask ourselves individually or that we, as a community of believers, ask collectively. For instance, in our current climate within the evangelical church in the United States, some questions we seem to be asking (or at least the questions we are asking that get a lot of attention) are:

- How might evangelical Christians come together to keep the United States from falling into moral decay?
- How can we preserve traditional Christian (American? Conservative?) values as we shift from one generation to the next?
- How can we retain the systems and structures that have been the staple of the evangelical, church growth, and mega-church movements over the past several decades?
- How might we preserve a culture in which our children will not suffer loss for being Christian?

Whether I have rightly identified these questions or not would surely depend on one's perspective on the evangelical church and its general disposition toward major cultural and generational shifts. I would freely admit that this list of questions may be wrong and is certainly incomplete. That said, even if I have all of the above questions wrong (or if you simply disagree with them), I do not often (enough) find evidence of the church asking more theological questions like:

- How might I/we surrender our rights or preferences in order to promote the unity of the body of Christ?

- How might my/our actions, words, or attitudes offer faithful testimony to who God is and what He has done?

- Who do I/we really want to be in this particular situation?

- How might we hand down our faith to the coming generations urging them to retain the vital linkage with historic Christian confession while allowing them the flexibility to "own" and "adapt" the faith to convey God faithfully in a context differently complex than our own?

- What might it look like for me/us to live as if I/we believe Matthew 6:30-34?

These latter questions are challenging for at least three reasons:

First, they resist settled, final answers. They resist any sort of settled, final answer because of the complex situations in which the questions are necessarily posed. For instance, the initial question concerning the promotion of Christian unity might be answered differently when considering whether or not to eat food sacrificed to idols (cf. Rom 15:20-23; 1 Cor 8:1-13) than when engaging in a public discussion about theological topics such as social justice or doctrinal drift. While the answers may be different, the heart of the question remains the same: how might I/we act in a manner that brings the body of Christ together in love and truth?

Second, the questions cannot be answered by appealing to one Bible verse or another *without simultaneously ignoring other Bible verses*. The questions do not allow us to stop at whether a particular combination of words and deeds are "biblical," but require us to choose between a variety of appropriate, biblically aligned words and deeds. In other words, they are not questions about permission (is the way I'm acting allowable according to the scriptures) but about wisdom (within the set of allowable actions and words I/we have at my/our disposal which will most faithfully render God in this specific situation). The questions demand more from us than to attach our actions to a specific Bible verse. They require us to tailor our words and deeds…to exercise wisdom…within the diverse situations in which we find ourselves.

Third, the questions are challenging because they require us to resist the impulse to create factions or assign blame. These questions demand a great deal of patience and humility…a willingness to listen well to one another and a commitment to living together in peace. Because they are not final or settled and cannot be decisively answered through appeal to a particular Bible verse, these questions (and others like them) serve to highlight the challenges we face when seeking to embody God's wisdom in a volatile, fallen environment where any number of "right" or "allowable" choices may be available to us.

Asking different questions is not a self-help strategy. I don't anticipate that it will make our individual or collective lives any easier. I would, however, anticipate that asking different questions will help us to become a more faithful, unified community. In asking new questions, we open ourselves up to new answers. We begin to reorient ourselves within the world so that we gain new perspective. That reorientation so changes our perspective that we become capable of speaking, acting, and being in the world in theologically faithful ways that were not possible before we asked the questions. Building our capacity to ask theological questions of the world around us and to consider how we might offer faithful Christian testimony within it, provides a means of cultivating the Christian mind that embraces the complexity of our context without decoupling us from the enduring truths of our faith.

<u>Considering Systems</u>

In Whitman's "Song of Myself" he writes,

"Do I contradict myself?

Very well then….I contradict myself

I am large….I contain multitudes."[94]

In this case, poetry, as it so often does, expresses the truth of a matter in an uncomplicated, yet profound manner. Like Whitman, each of us is "large." Our communities are "large." We (both individually and collectively) contain contradictions, tensions, and ambiguities. We may be large, but God is vast. If we are incapable of understanding ourselves well enough to resolve the contradictions that exist within us, we are surely incapable of grasping fully the vastness of God who exists without contradiction. So, as we consider systems, we must recognize both our limited capacity for comprehension and our inability to be "large" without contradiction.

We exist within a series of overlapping systems, which "function to preserve communal boundaries, societal order, and *stability*."[95] As such, systems help us to navigate and impose order upon the complex and chaotic world around us. As Thiselton notes regarding a hermeneutics of doctrine, however, "the notion of a 'final' system is excluded."[96] Instead, "there is room for 'system' both as coherence…and as a provision for boundary markers and identity markers in interaction with ongoing history, experience, and hermeneutical life-worlds."[97]

As we consider the broader systems in which we participate, our goal is "to step back from our patterns and habits about thinking about the world and instead be more intentional and explicit about the way we approach a problem or situation—especially when it comes to the complexity of the situation."[98] For those seeking to cultivate a Christian mind it is crucial that, as we are "more intentional and explicit about the way we approach a problem or situation," we do so in a manner that reflects a faithful understanding of God. The systems in which we participate, even the Christian systems, are not "final." Instead, they are incomplete and malleable seeking to sustain themselves "through demarcation from and adaptation to a changeable, hypercomplex environment."[99]

As we begin to consider systems, we recognize that our goal cannot simply be to master the disciplines of biblical and theological studies.[100] While these disciplines surely offer benefits, they too are systems of a sort. As such, they are incomplete and incapable of providing a full and final picture of God and the world. It is not that there is no enduring truth. Jesus will never be something other than God and man, the Old Testament (despite some recent treatments) will never become obsolete, and salvation will never come through anything but faith alone. Pledging solidarity to a given system…even systems as beneficial as those of biblical and theological studies…creates obligations that "come to be invoked in the form of insistence on compliance with certain common rules."[101]

Rather than adhering to a particular system, a Christian mind recognizes the necessity of navigating multiple systems in light of the God revealed in the scriptures. Far from developing a set of black and white rules that govern the manner in which we interact with the world, considering systems requires a different sort of conformity. We are released to pursue this conformity…a conformity to the order of God's kingdom.

In other words, rather than interacting with the various systems in which we participate from the standpoint of the world, we participate from the standpoint of God's revelation. The pinnacle of that revelation is found in the events of Christ's sinless life, sacrificial death, and triumphal resurrection. As O'Donovan notes,

> "…these aspects of abnegation and transcendence in personal ethics, of criticism and revolution in social ethics, are prevented from becoming negative and destructive by the fact that they are interpreted from the centre, the confirmation of the world-order which God has made. Man's life on earth is important to God; he has given it its order; it matters that it should conform to the order he has given it. Once we have grasped that, we can understand too how this order requires of us both a denial of all that threatens to become disordered and a progress towards a life which goes beyond this order without negating it."[102]

We cannot escape the systems in which we participate, nor do we need to do so. Our participation in the systems of the world is part of our vocation…part of the commitment we make in following Christ. As Paul says, "I have been crucified with Christ. It is no longer I who live, but Christ who lives in me. And the life I now live in the flesh I live by faith in the Son of God, who loved me and gave himself for me" (Gal 2:20). Paul continues to live in the world, but does not exist in the world in the same manner as he did prior to his death to the law. In a similar manner, we continue as participants in the world, yet we do so as those who understand that the present age is passing away.

Cultivating a Christian mind within a set of overlapping, complex systems, then, requires that we commit to standing with integrity by refusing to place any identity above our identity in Christ. Part of that identity involves something akin to what Snowden calls "emergence." In his work on the Cynefin framework, Snowden describes the challenges leaders face within complex contexts in which "right answers can't be ferreted out."[103] It is "the realm of 'unknown unknowns'."[104] Within this realm, Snowden recommends that "instead of attempting to impose a course of action, leaders must patiently allow the path forward to reveal itself."[105] Complex contexts heighten the temptation to "overcontrol" and to "preempt the opportunity for informative patterns to emerge."[106]

If we, as members of the body of Christ, are indeed in a complex situation, we must resist the temptation to "fall back into traditional command-and-control" orientations to the world.[107] Instead, we must allow solutions to emerge as we walk faithfully with our God. Rather than taking it upon ourselves to solve a problem, we take it upon ourselves to be "a stone amid the waves; wet, yet unimpressed" by the storm raging around us.[108] Christians must continue to act in the world, yet they must act as women and men who understand that their actions need not be effective to be faithful.

Christian action in the world need not be limited to any one sort, yet it cannot exclude those activities that are constitutive of Christian identity.

Confession of sin, love for the brethren, unceasing prayer, participation in worship, and a host of other actions are non-negotiable for the Christian community. As we engage in Christian practice…living out our identity as the body of Christ…we will find ourselves better prepared to deal with complexity and to allow God's solutions to emerge.

<u>Developing into Expert Christians</u>

Memory, particularly in educational circles, has taken something of a backseat to understanding or, perhaps worse, exposure. Survey courses such as Old Testament Survey and New Testament Survey are included in almost every Christian college, Bible college, and seminary curricula. Many of these require students to read the whole Bible (or large sections of it) throughout the course of a given semester. While reading Scripture is seldom a "bad" thing to do, there is a gap between exposure to the text and understanding the text. Bridging that gap may well involve some sort of retrieval practice.[109]

In suggesting memorization as a technique necessary to cultivate a Christian mind, I am not advocating for every Christian to sit down and commit the whole Bible to memory. At the same time, it seems clear that "retrieval practice—recalling facts or concepts or events from memory—is a more effective learning strategy than review by rereading."[110] The goal of this sort of recall is not "mindless recitation," but to develop reflexes so that more basic knowledge and skills can be leveraged and applied creatively within a given situation. One need not choose between memory and creativity. Rather, "…as knowledge amounts to little without the exercise of ingenuity and imagination, creativity absent a sturdy foundation of knowledge builds a shaky house."[111]

To the extent that cultivating a Christian mind involves learning (and I believe that it does to a large extent), it seems appropriate for Christians to become good learners so that the Christian knowledge and skills we have at our disposal can be "readily available from memory" and used to "make sense of future problems and opportunities."[112] Building a ever-expanding reservoir of biblical knowledge and Christian discipline upon which we can draw as we (a) approach the challenges of the day, (b) reflect on our actions, and (c) redirect our impulses toward faithfulness, becomes an ongoing activity that transcends (though it may involve) one's daily time of devotion.

Such a reservoir is created through a diverse array of disciplines practiced so often that they become second nature. Wells speaks to the development of this sort of "second nature" distinguishing between "the time for moral effort" and "the time of formation and training:"

> "Training requires commitment, discipline, faithfulness, study, apprenticeship, practice, cooperation, observation, reflection—in short, moral effort. The point of this effort is to form skills and habits—habits that mean people take the right things for granted and skills that give them ability to do the things they take for granted. The time for moral habit is the 'moment of decision'...In every moral 'situation,' the real decisions are ones that have been taken some time before...no amount of effort at the moment of decision will make up for effort neglected in the time of formation."[113]

Developing a commitment to training and preparation that results in Christians taking "the right things for granted" and giving us the "ability to do the things" we take for granted, is what becoming an expert Christian is about at its core. We need to strive to become expert Christians rather than becoming Christian experts. There is a subtle difference between the two. In the latter case, Christians are capable of portraying themselves as experts on a variety of topics. Christian experts can, for instance, convey a knowledge of the scriptures and of theology while simultaneously bludgeoning those who would dare to oppose them. Christian experts can become too narrowly focused on their particular area of expertise that they ignore the virtues of grace, humility, and charity. In other words, Christian experts form habits commensurate with particular disciplines and operate in accordance with those disciplines rather than in accordance with the scriptures.

Expert Christians, on the other hand, do not see a particular expertise in some skill or area of knowledge as anything but a gift of God used to glorify

Him. Expert Christians internalize the scriptures, the core practices of the Christian faith, and the doctrines of the church so that they more naturally respond to and engage the world as Christians. This internalization is not voluntary, but commensurate with a primary Christian identity. In other words, to be Christian without such internalization is to make what it means to be a Christian unintelligible. Expert Christians recognize that embodiment…the enfleshing of the body of Christ through individual and corporate testimony to the reign of God…is not a means to an end, but an end in itself.

Such expert Christians are not tucked away from the world, but exist within the world as a people of distinction…as a people whose wise actions and reactions look "foolish" (1 Cor 4:10). As Fitch suggests,

> "If the church is the social body of His Lordship (His in-breaking Reign) incarnating Christ in the world for God's mission it must not be segregated into a gathering on Sunday morning. The church must be present as Christ in neighborhoods. It must gather to be present among the hungry and hurting, however that might look. This means the practice of the church must be decentralized in its organization away from one central place to being present in the everyday lives of the people."[114]

Expert Christians recognize the Lordship of God and make Christ visible to the world by (a) developing habits and (b) engaging in deliberate practice. As Clear notes, "…when you want to maximize your potential and achieve elite levels of performance…You can't repeat the same things blindly and expect to become exceptional. Habits are necessary, but not sufficient for mastery. What you need is a combination of automatic habits and deliberate practice."[115] He goes on to note, "Mastery is the process of narrowing your focus to a tiny element of success, repeating it until you have internalized the skill, and then using this new habit as the foundation to advance to the next frontier of your development."[116]

Expert Christians don't just emerge. It is an effortful process that involves commitment to living out an identity deeply rooted not in human strategies or tactics, but in our essential being as adoptive children of God. Such an identity is forged through individual and communal practices of prayer, study, and the discernment of the Spirit's activity in the world. Expert Christians enact the scriptures and the doctrines of the church within the missional spaces in which God is already at work. Participating with God in His mission means that we take the opportunity to embrace "the sacred occasion for Christ to be incarnated further into the world."[117] To be ready to do so, we must have participated in and as a community that shapes our habits and dispositions, as well as challenging us not to be creatures of habit, but to become masters of the craft of being Christian.

Conclusion

Cultivating a Christian mind is no easy task. It requires commitment, humility, and, perhaps most of all, an ongoing willingness to remain available to God and to the leading of the Holy Spirit. We do not lose ourselves in the disciplines and community of the church. Practicing prayer, participating in worship, taking communion, submitting to the scriptures, giving to support God's missional activity become less like paying taxes and more like breathing. In other words, they are not the activities in which we engage because ignoring them has consequences we would rather avoid (like not paying taxes). Instead, they are practices that become so natural and necessary that not doing them feels suffocating…as if something within us is broken.

Building a set of strategies to listen to others (and to the Other), ask different questions, consider systems, and develop into expert Christians, begins to open us up to the possibilities of God. They begin to free us from the constraints of our own limitations and the limitations of our communities by broadening our perspective about what God is doing in the world, how we might best participate, and why the reasons we might have for not joining with God in mission are "light and momentary" in comparison to the "eternal glory that far outweighs them all" (2 Cor 4:17).

5 Public Christian Testimony

Introduction

I first discovered Maryanne Wolf's *Proust and the Squid: The Story and Science of the Reading Brain* while doing research for an essay entitled "Old Testament Theology and the Digital Age."[118] Wolf, unlike some other writers who have examined reading in a digital age, sees the potential pitfalls *and* benefits new technologies bring. Perhaps the most compelling aspect of her work is that it begins with the simple insight that "human beings were never born to read."[119] As Wolf notes regarding the development of the reading brain, "…we rearranged the very organization of our brain, which in turn expanded the way we were able to think…"[120] While the human brain, according to Wolf, had to develop the neural networks to read, she contends (as would I) that the reading brain is something we can lose or, at least, diminish in ways that could be quite unfortunate.

In "Old Testament Theology and the Digital Age," I raise concerns related to the potential degradation of long-form reading ability, as well as the need for the discipline of Old Testament theology to "take into account the challenges of cultivating sustained, deep thinking in relation to any topic, including Old Testament theology, in the digital age."[121] I also recommend that for Old Testament theology to adapt to a digital age there will likely be a need for Old Testament theologians to "participate through new, digital forms of societal discourse" and to be Old Testament theologians in the public square. This new participation is largely based on the recognition that "the next generation of men and women may well be less than likely or less than prepared to read academic works, sit in seminary classrooms, or even attend a Sunday service."[122] My aim was to speak to future Old Testament theologians and to highlight some of the challenges that might face the academic discipline of Old Testament theology in the future.

As I began the research for this essay, I was pleased to find that Maryanne Wolf has continued her research and published a new book entitled *Reader, Come Home: The Reading Brain in a Digital World*. I have also broadened the scope of my inquiry from the reading brain and Old Testament theology to the role of discourse in the formation of the Christian mind. Our minds are being shaped through the ways in which we interact through technology and, increasingly, the ways in which technology interacts with us. As such, works like Eli Pariser's *The Filter Bubble*, Kahnemann's *Thinking, Fast and Slow*, Bostrom's *Superintelligence*, and various other works have served as crucial conversation partners.[123] To offer a bit of foreshadowing, this essay is about the ways in which the digital age is uniquely structuring and influencing our thinking and decision making and how Christians might create space for deeper, richer Christian thought and discourse within it.

Describing Discourse

While the digital age is not a demon that must be exorcised from the Christian community, it has positive and negative implications that must be taken into account. The Christian community is and will always be a community whose identity is formed by the scriptures. As such, the community of faith must preserve and cultivate some sort of literacy that will allow for a "deep reading" of, or deep engagement with, the biblical text and the various works of theology produced by faithful men and women throughout the history of the church.[124] Deep reading is reading of the sort that "requires human beings to call upon and develop attentional skills, to be thoughtful and fully aware."[125] It is "the slow and meditative possession of a book."[126]

Whatever benefits the digital age offers, it brings with it the danger of dulling the sort of literacy that encourages "deep reading."

Yet, the Christian mind requires more than simply the ability to read deeply. After all, before one can read a work of literature deeply, one must choose the work of literature to be read. Reading is not simply a matter of neurological ability, nor is choosing a particular literary work done apart from external influences. Instead, reading is *one* means of participating in the particular discourses of the social groups of which one is a part. These discourses in the form of literary (and other) works arise from particular cultural settings past and present. Literature is a part of culture and, as such, cannot be fully understood apart from the past influences that informed a given literary work, the cultural milieu in which it was produced, and the contemporary situations to which a literary work currently speaks. As Bahktin notes, "If it is impossible to study literature apart from an epoch's entire culture, it is even more fatal to encapsulate a literary phenomenon in the single epoch of its creation, in its own contemporaneity…"[127] Literary works are born of cultures and sub-cultures that are tied into the discourses of the past and that rethink, expand, or otherwise modify those discourses in the present.

If it is the case that reading is indeed a means of participating in particular discourses, it seems appropriate to consider the nature of discourse and the means through which we, as individual and collective participants, choose (or end up conforming unreflectively to) the implicit rules of a discourse and the power it exercises over us. Fairclough, for instance, addresses the linkage between language and power, particularly the "exercise of power through the manufacture of consent."[128] At one point, he notes, that "social control" is often "practised [*sic*]…through consent" so that people are immersed "into apparatuses of control which they come to feel themselves to be a part of (e.g. as consumers or as owners of shares in the 'share-owning democracy')."[129] Fairclough represents discourse as "language use conceived of as socially determined."[130] Discourse becomes a mechanism influencing and framing language and thought.[131]

Chouliaraki and Fairclough also describes discourse in terms of practices or "habitualised [sic] ways, tied to particular times and places, in which people apply resources (material or symbolic) to act together in the world."[132] Discourse understood as a particular instance of social practice embedded within a complex network of other social practices is both influential and malleable. Discourse does have an influence over the ways that we speak and think, yet it is not an oppressive beast from which there is no escape. Human agency is not lost through discourse, nor does discourse leave human agency to roam without boundary or constraint. Discourse offers a flow of consciousness across generations and cultures in which we participate (or not) by choice and circumstance.

One may think of discourse, then as both a structure and a practice. It is a structure in so much as the normal conventions of language and the topics addressed as part of a particular political, social, academic, or legal field are largely assumed and exhibit a degree of resilience while retaining pliability. Discourse as structure does not control thought, nor does it demand a particular way of conversing and interacting. Instead, as a structure, discourse represents, to one extent or another, an ongoing agreement (or consent) to remain within the norms set by a particular order of discourse.

Discourse may also be understood as a practice. Even within the context of a discourse structure, individual actors or groups of actors can exercise agency to participate in that discourse structure in ways that modify the discourse in some manner. Discourse as practice allows individuals and groups to "play in the margins" by exploring a discourse's previously neglected aspects. This dynamic aligns well with Bahktin's description of discourse as "polyphonic" and the necessity to thread the needle between relativism and dogmatism, which "equally exclude all argumentation, all authentic dialogue, by making it unnecessary (relativism) or impossible (dogmatism)."[133] It may be helpful then to think of discourse through a structural-practice heuristic. Discourse as structure constrains (though not absolutely), whereas discourse as practice creates space for originality and quests for truth (though within limits). We participate in discourse when we properly negotiate and work within the constraints while pursuing truth through rigorous dialogue.[134]

Discourse in a Digital Age

Surely the digital world in which we live amplifies the degree of influence particular discourses have on us as individuals and groups. As Pariser notes, "Your identity shapes your media, and your media then shapes what you believe and what you care about. You click on a link, which signals an interest in something, which means you're more likely to see articles about the topic in the future, which in turn prime the topic for you. You become trapped in a you loop, and if your identity is misrepresented, strange patterns begin to emerge…"[135] This "you loop" is deceptive when we don't recognize (a) that we are in it or (b) that we need to step out of it.

If we continually have our own perceptions, urges, instincts, preferences, or "expertise" (what we currently "know" about the world or a particular topic) reinforced through the narrowing of the amount of information we are able to access, we run the risk of becoming entrenched and dismissive of opposing views of the world. Our brains, or particular operations within them, seek out coherence. According to Kahneman, mental operations may be divided into an intuitive operation ("Type 1" or "System 1") and a more contemplative operation ("Type 2" or "System 2"). These operations are not equally yoked. Instead, "the intuitive System 1 is more influential than your experience tells you, and it is the secret author of many of the choices and judgments you make."[136]

The more intuitive, "system 1" mental operations privilege coherence, which "means that you're going to adopt one interpretation in general. Ambiguity tends to be suppressed."[137] System 1 "is part of the mechanism that you have here that ideas activate other ideas, and the more coherent they are, the more likely they are to activate each other. Other things that don't fit fall by the wayside. We're enforcing coherent interpretation."[138] While it is often beneficial to assume coherence and suppress ambiguity, there are also times when defaulting to coherence and suppressing ambiguity limits our ability to thicken and make more complex the stories we tell ourselves.

The information available to us (or more readily available to us) creates availability biases through which we make judgements based only on the information we have without taking into account the information we don't.[139] Perhaps worse, in its quest for coherence, the System 1 operations not only squeeze out ambiguous information or information that does not support the construction of a coherent story, it does so with little regard for the "amount and quality of the data on which the story is based."[140]

System 2 is more effortful and, despite the normal dominance of System 1 operations, "has some ability to change the way System 1 works, by programming the normally automatic functions of attention and memory."[141] Our brain does not work against us, but it is not an infallible ally. The way we make decisions and form judgments creates a particular perception of the way the world works. We must trust our brain even as we learn to challenge it.

Prior to the onset of the digital age, we were not pristine in our thoughts or uninfluenced by media. Media has traditionally served as a means of influencing our behavior through marketing, reinforcing values through books and curricula, or cultivating social identities across time. We have always had a limited capacity for information processing and a limited access to information more generally. In this respect, the digital age is not altogether different from the pre-digital age.

We were susceptible to media through "analog" selectivity filters well before Google, Amazon, or Facebook began collecting data, making recommendations, or personalizing our searches and news feeds. While the filtering and personalization employed by digital entities may appear to be more systemic and disciplined (perhaps even more pernicious), they are not new. They are a sharpening and expansion of underlying logics and strategies that have been employed with various other media in times past.

Take, for instance, traditional publishing. Publishing houses do not publish everything, nor do they choose books to publish at random. They publish books that they believe will have a solid readership and/or that make a contribution to a particular discourse. In other words, publishers serve as a filter for the material that is put in print for us to read. Based on the success of a particular book or author, publishing houses make judgments about what the reading public will want to read next and, thus, what will sell. They also make decisions about what conversations should be happening by publishing works that they believe are, in some way, important.

Similarly, a sixty minute radio broadcast makes choices by selecting what constitutes the important news of the day. By choosing what constitutes the most important news, broadcasters filter information and, to one degree or another, shape or reinforce our interests. The voices that the broadcasters choose to speak to a particular issue become the expert voices enjoying not only popularity but the perception (or misperception) that they speak authoritatively as "keepers of a tradition" whose thinking on an issue is beyond critique or disagreement.[142] There can develop an impression that they represent the only viable perspective on a given issue. In reality, experts (and everyone else) frames descriptions and explanations in particular ways that can have an impact on the way in which information is received and understood.[143]

Based on the examples of publishing and radio, it seems clear that selection of content and the manner in which issues are framed have a rather significant influence on readers and listeners. Choosing the topics that will be addressed and framing conversations gave (and continue to give) more traditional media entities the power to set the "conversational agenda" in a manner similar to a Google algorithm.[144] Surely the dynamics of the digital age are different in a number of ways, but it would be naïve to think that we have somehow moved from a pristine period of unfiltered information to one in which all information has become inherently tainted. In fact, the digital age is not without its upside.

For instance, in a pre-digital age, "minority reports" or opinions outside of the mainstream, were more difficult to access. Stories released were conditioned by a host of factors including, but not limited to, perceived consumer interest, judgments of the intelligentsia, academic elites, and other gatekeepers (e.g. editors, producers, etc.), as well as the general structure of discourse and the moment in time in which a piece of literature, article, or other form of media was produced. The digital age removes many, if not all, of the barriers previously controlled by professional gatekeepers, as well as limiting concerns regarding space and time. These changes allow for a massive increase in the amount of published "minority reports" and diverse perspectives across multiple different media.

Unleashing more information is beneficial to the extent that such information can leverage cognitive diversity which consists of diverse perspectives, interpretations, heuristics, and predictive models.[145] The mere *presence* of diverse perspectives, however, does not guarantee *interaction* with diverse perspectives. In their study of group decision making, Stasser and Titus found two biases:

> "First, discussion is biased in favor of shared information: An item of information is more likely to enter discussion if it is shared rather than unshared. Second, discussion is biased in favor of the current preferences of group members: An item of information is more likely to enter discussion if it favors rather than opposes the existent preferences of group members."[146]

These two biases have the potential to effectively counteract the benefits of diverse knowledge and perspectives within a group, as well as pointing to the role of preference in decision making for judgmental tasks.[147]

Beyond decision making, certain media studies suggest that attitudes and identities are reinforced by access and exposure to media consistent with one's existing attitudes and identities. These same studies suggest that one's existing attitudes and identities predispose the choice of media consistent with those attitudes and identities.[148] The Reinforcing Spiral Model "develops the idea of media content exposure being both cause and effect of various attitudes about oneself and about the social world."[149] In other words, we are less likely to choose media *inconsistent* with our existing attitudes and identities, particularly as such attitudes and identities become more entrenched or, perhaps, when there is a perceived threat to one's social identity. As Slater notes, "…selectivity of attitude- and identity-consistent content are likely to operate only to the extent necessary to maintain a reasonable level of comfort with respect to protecting identity-central attitudes and beliefs."[150] We tend to choose media and gravitate toward perspectives that reinforce our existing understandings of the world around us to the extent needed to retain and reinforce our "identity-central attitudes and beliefs."[151]. We also tend to minimize our exposure to content that would represent a major challenge to our existing attitudes and beliefs when we feel they may bring about a crisis in identity.

Beyond the individual and social mechanisms that influence our media choices, new filtering strategies employed by search engines and the like exist, in part, to help manage the ever increasing amount of material available in the digital world. Such filtering is not altogether bad. After all, "too many options are just as problematic as too few—you can find yourself over-whelmed by the number of options or paralyzed by the paradox of choice."[152] The issue, then, is not the act of filtering *per se*, but the reinforcing effect that current filtering methods have on our thinking and on our ability to engage with novel ideas and diverse perspectives.[153] It becomes more and more difficult to escape a particular order of discourse or to engage that discourse in a critical manner because we already agree with most of what we are reading. In one sense, discourse in the digital age becomes more monologue than dialogue. We may be hearing new stories, but those stories often serve to reinforce our pre-existing views of the world rather than pushing us to see the world in new ways.

Christian Literacies for the Digital Age

Deep reading is not the "silver bullet fix" for the issues here described. It is necessary, but not sufficient. Reading deeply works that promote coherence interpretation and only serve to reinforce (or further entrench) pre-existing attitudes and identities will not necessarily challenge our established notions about a particular topic or the world in general. Instead, we must reconsider certain fundamental assumptions about how we challenge our mental frameworks, explore new topics, and become more savvy in our engagement with what might generally be considered standard discourse.[154] We must develop new literacies…Christian literacies…adapted to the digital age. Part of these new Christian literacies is recognizing the difference between surrendering to the selective process involved in a particular discourse and accepting that selective process while interrogating what has been said and seeking to discern what has been left out.

For instance, this essay is divided into subheadings to offer clarity regarding the broad topics I have chosen to address. My hope is that they will help readers better understand my analysis. I recognize (as should you!) that in selecting my topics and sub-topics, I have determined what is important and am representing to you that the topics I have chosen are more important (perhaps more supportive of my broader agenda?) than other topics. Such an admission on my part should not be a new revelation. I certainly have an agenda and come at this work from an interested perspective.

However, in recognizing that my work is both structured and incomplete, I also recognize that it is not the final word on these matters, nor should you assume I have spoken it. I seek to make a contribution to the broader dialogue on Christian thought…not to offer a comprehensive tome (if that were even possible). You should not be reading this work without also asking yourself where I am mistaken, where I have overstated (or understated) my case, whether my reading of the research is appropriate, how I have jumped too quickly to conclusions, or when I have left out pertinent topics that you feel could have been included to advance or nuance my analysis. Writing about some of the biases and tendencies toward reinforcing pre-existing notions doesn't mean that I will avoid them at every (or perhaps any) turn.

In speaking of Christian literacies for a digital age, I am attempting to understand those literacies as practices that occur within the community of faith. While I will say far less than could be said on these matters, I wish to highlight a particular skill that, it seems to me, we are losing as we participate in the various discourses of the digital age. In speaking of Christian literacy (or literacies), I am not solely concerned with the ability of the brain to decode (read) or produce (write) texts. While such skills are, important given that the Christian community is committed to being a people committed to a God who revealed himself in the scriptures, we cannot assume that this important skill is also a sufficient skill, especially when embedded within the body of Christ in its diverse cultural, geographic, and social settings. Christian literacy, includes, but is not defined by, an ability to read the Bible or otherwise engage with the word of God. Instead, Christian literacy must include a critical understanding of the impact technology and culture have on Christian media production and consumption more generally.

Certain studies of "new literacy" support this understanding. The field of new literacy studies is itself highly diverse offering less-than uniform definitions of what actually constitutes "new literacy." As Leu, et al. suggest, literacy is not a stable concept…it is not simply defined as one's capacity to read and write. Literacy is a moving target since what it means "to be literate tomorrow will be defined by even newer technologies that have yet to appear and even newer discourses and social practices that will be created to meet future needs."[155]

New literacy necessarily arises because literacy is not the "simple" act of reading and writing, but a situated skillset influenced by social and technological conditions. Commenting on the "literacy myth" Gee concludes,

> "People who take a sociocultural approach to literacy believe that the 'literacy myth'—the idea that literacy leads inevitably to a long list of 'good' things—is a 'myth' because literacy in and of itself, abstracted from historical conditions and social practices, has no effects, or, at least, no predictable effects. Rather, what has effects are historically and culturally

situated social practices of which reading and writing are only bits, bits that are differently composed and situated in different social practices."[156]

Gee's point is that being able to decode words on a page is not the gateway to enlightenment that many people might assume. It may certainly be a necessary skill set, but, abstracted from a historical and social situation in which reading and writing is a necessary skill set`, being literate is not the end all, be all of human existence. Instead, we need to consider the ability to read and write as a social practice in networked relation to other social practices that together allow us to navigate particular historical and cultural moments.[157]

While it is crucial to the formation of Christian social identity to continually interact with the scriptures, it is equally important to reinforce such interactions through participation in social practices intended to deepen one's sense of Christian social identity. Within the digital realm, Christian literacies will almost certainly include skillsets similar to those needed in the era of analog (or before). While the criteria and decision process may look different in different epochs or cultures, there has been and will likely continue to be a need to exercise discernment with regard to the information consumed.[158]

At the same time, the current digital environment requires a great deal of responsibility that was, in times past, largely shouldered by cultural gatekeepers. Christians can publish anything online they choose without any requirement for accountability or oversight. Misleading, incomplete, or wholly false information is no longer subject to review, nor is it necessarily open to critique or dialogue in any true sense of the word. In the digital world, we not only need to exercise discernment with regard to the information we consume, but constraint and wisdom with regard to the information we produce and present. We do not speak, publish, and post as individuals…we do so as members of the body of Christ and it is to the body that we must be accountable.

Conclusion: Christian Testimony and the Christian Mind

What does this all mean for the Christian mind? **First**, the Christian mind is a situated mind. It participates in a variety of discourse structures and discourse practices. Recognizing that such discourses are often supported through the "manufacture of consent" rather than occurring within an unfiltered space is important. One example might be Hunter's discussion of the politicization of Christian thought in which many thinkers have, to one degree or another, overemphasized the political aspects of Christianity accepting the broader ethos of American political mechanisms.[159] As "the political" begins to dominate the broader landscape of discourse, understandings of the church as a political entity and a political actor become more common. Political solutions tend to take center stage as they are assumed to be the most logical and effective solutions to the problems of society. The Christian mind cannot surrender this ground. The political and governmental arenas have their place, but they do not drive the agenda for the church.

Similarly, one might also note "justice" warriors of various stripes who feel it is their divine calling to make public the failings of various Christian leaders. While the Christian mind demands accountability, the sort of journalism and social media activity that seems to garner the most attention is often ungracious, under-informed, and framed as a sort of "anti-PR" message.[160] Whatever the place of journalists ends up being in the digital world, it is difficult to disagree with Stephens who notes, "Journalism that leaps out ahead of the evidence, that is surer than it has reason to be sure, that pontificates, spouts, hazards guesses, or 'tells' when it is indeed 'too soon to tell' is not the kind of journalism I see leading the way out of the current crisis."[161]

Accountability is necessary and good, but we cannot simply assume that social media is an appropriate medium through which to exercise Christian accountability. In other words, elevating the appropriate concerns for accountability, justice, and "prophetic speech" above other legitimate theological concerns would seem to ignore the challenges associated with our tendencies toward coherent stories and our willingness to accept evidence (even poor evidence) when it reinforces our pre-existing perspectives.

Second, the Christian mind rejects systems and structures that curtail its appropriate imagination. While the individual human brain will always have to make choices about the nature and volume of information it engages, the Christian mind is not simply housed inside the skulls of individual Christians. It is also a "composite" mind forged through dialogue and difference unified in Christ. Internet filters and the participation in discourses that serve to reinforce our perspectives on the world subtly challenge the agency of the Christian mind. The situation is not altogether dire as the Christian mind can still choose to exercise agency and to dig into new topics or confront new challenges. However, the exercise of such agency does not necessarily mean that the Christian mind is free from dominant forms of discourse. Christians must be consistently diligent to guard against discourses that limit our theological imagination by closing off new thinking and polarizing positions that do not do justice to the complexity of the issue at hand.

Finally, the Christian mind is oriented toward community, which means that we are not simply representing one case or another, but participating in an ongoing, multi-generational, multi-ethnic dialogue and all of the cognitive differences that come with it. Doggedly holding to one orientation or perspective while demeaning or demonizing others (pointing out their flaws while suggesting that your perspective has none) is not in keeping with the Christian mind. The research noted above and several other works that have informed my thinking on these matters suggest that we are in danger of losing dialogue. Not interaction (we still have plenty of that), but dialogue.

When we cannot have a true exchange of ideas designed to more fully grasp the truth, the Christian mind will be at a greater risk of atrophy.[162] While I don't know that I have proved this point in the analysis above, I am concerned that the Christian mind is being lost, in part, because we have forgotten that we are members of the body of Christ…members of the church…and that church is about more than demanding perfection.

Orienting the Christian mind toward community, would, in my estimation, require a rethinking of the current evangelical situation in which the big voices of popular preachers or Christian leaders "represent" evangelical perspective on a variety of matters and create the categories through which the Christian mind "must" think in order to be classified as Christian. In my estimation, this phenomenon is not a symptom (solely) of individual arrogance or expertise, but one emerging from a weak ecclesiology that has not taken the time to engage in dialogue with the diverse array of individuals that God has called together for his glory.

6 Responsible Christian Testimony

Introduction

As writing this series of essays might imply, I believe academic writing to be within the appropriate range of activities in which a Christian mind might engage. However, as the title of this particular essay suggests, I have my concerns about the nature of public testimony in the present day and the role certain media and media personalities should play (if any) in calling to account Christian leaders and organizations. In addition, I am less confident than some that certain analog and digital environments offer spaces capable of sustaining genuine engagement with ideas or offering a fair hearing of multiple sides of an issue.[163] Digital conversation often becomes polarized with groups holding differing perspectives talking past each other. Dissenting opinions can often be met with disdain if not hostility as affinity groups pull together to support one another rather than to test, try, and strengthen their perspectives on the world.

Group interactions and dialogue aside, my primary concern in this essay is related to authorship. I am particularly concerned with critical reports that levy accusations at Christian leaders and organizations. To be clear, I am not denying the power of the pen in certain instances. I would not disallow criticism…even public criticism…as an activity appropriate to a Christian mind. Nor would I deny that there are Christian leaders and ministries engaged in practices that lack integrity.[164] Instead, I am calling into question what constitutes responsible Christian testimony in public and how the digital age impacts the means and limits of such testimony.

The Responsible Author

Before addressing the issue of testimony specifically, it will be important to have at least a preliminary sense of the theological responsibilities of authors and the difference a Christian mind might make to one's approach to authorship. In particular, the following discussion will focus on the role of Christian authors in the analysis and reporting of current events involving accusations against Christian leaders or organizations of moral impropriety, incompetence, theological drift, and the like. Christian authors seeking to investigate and report on such matters take on a heavy responsibility to ensure that, in calling leaders to account, they do not themselves exert an influence that wrongly wounds other members of the body of Christ without being held accountable for that damage.

Some might argue that when morally and theologically corrupt Christian leaders and institutions are allowed to operate without sufficient accountability, the Christian "fourth estate" has a responsibility to use media to bring the truth to light. Yet, I am suspicious about the capacity of contemporary forms of media and those who use them to represent faithfully the complexities of present-day situations. My academic background and interactions with those who engage in detailed historical analysis suggest to me that those who criticize leaders and organizations in the present day have often failed to engage in the sort of rigorous investigations necessary to render a contemporary situation with sufficient depth. Too often accounts seem to assume that the underlying causes of a particular situation are self-evident when, in fact, they may be far more opaque.

This lack of depth is partially due to an overemphasis on the present "crisis." Within such a crisis, the voices of a particularly aggrieved individual or group tend to dominate. The more angst conjured up by the current crisis, the easier it is to view leaders as incompetent (at best) and immoral (at worst). As Kahneman notes, "We are prone to blame decision makers for good decisions that worked out badly and to give them too little credit for successful moves that appear obvious only after the fact. There is a clear *outcome bias*."[165] While leaders are responsible for the outcomes of the decisions they make, there is a difference between (a) immoral action, (b) incompetence, (c) the inability to control all the factors that influence a particular outcome, and (d) intentional choices that result in less-than positive consequences.[166] When reports of present-day crises overemphasize the outcome of a series of decisions, they promote the outcome bias and diminish or ignore more ambiguous factors that contributed to the current state of affairs, as well as blaming or demeaning a particular leader by framing the current crisis as avoidable if only he or she were a competent, strategic, or moral leader.

Take an example from the fitness industry. I worked as a personal trainer for about five years in the late nineties and early two-thousands. My primary role was to work with clients in a one-on-one setting by designing workout routines that would help them achieve their fitness goals. I also offered coaching and advice on health and wellness more generally, as well as monitoring my clients' nutrition. Inevitably, some clients achieved their goals while others didn't.

At times, when a client didn't see the needle on the scale heading in the right direction, he or she blamed me. In part, I was responsible. They were paying me for results and the methods I was using to motivate and hold them accountable weren't working. The strategy I developed and the tactics I employed failed to help them reach their goals. At the same time, there were only so many factors I could control. After several different plans failed with one of my clients, for example, she went to the doctor and found that she had a hormone imbalance that was making it difficult for her to lose weight. It really wouldn't have mattered what program I developed…I couldn't fix her hormone issue. That factor was outside of my control.

The point is that while it can be comforting and easy to place blame, it is often inappropriate and unhelpful. Outcomes are not the only (or best) gage of a leader's competence or character in every situation. Other factors may well have contributed to a crisis situation. Similarly, when the problem is misdiagnosed due to a lack of rigor in reporting or insufficient knowledge of the situation, the wrong "problem" may be fixed, thus providing no real solution. Blaming the leader for an outcome, in other words, isn't always going to rectify the problem.

Giving in to outcome biases yields simple narratives that can and, from my perspective, often do dismiss the possibility of "counter-evidence." They lean too heavily on matters of observation without leaving open the possibility that new information might surface that shed new light on what seemed to be clear observations. In his discussion of natural testimony, Coady describes the challenge of "reports of particular facts of the sort which appear to favor the present suggestion: there are many cases in which the attested fact, said to be ultimately 'a matter of observation for somebody,' seems to be no such thing."[167] Coady also addresses "counter-evidence" with regard to formal testimony noting, "an audience may take it that a dispute no longer exists, a question is no longer open, and that they have legitimate certainty…yet be alive to the possibility that a further witness may cause the question to be re-opened and their certainty to diminish or disappear."[168]

In other words, there is a difference between an observation and an interpretation masquerading as an observation.[169] We may see a particular business outcome (e.g. a sharp drop in attendance or giving) or hear the complaints of certain members of the community and infer (or interpret) that the leader is doing something wrong. In reality, we must leave open the possibility that a drop in attendance is driven by factors other than leadership and that the dissatisfaction of community members may mean the leader is actually doing a good job.[170] We may have our suspicions about what is happening, but having suspicions and reporting suspicions (as fact) are quite different matters.

The point is that testimony and evidence are not as simple to handle as some may think, particularly when only a portion of the information regarding a situation is actually presented. Christians reporting on present-day events in the public eye take on the responsibility of offering a particular sort of testimony…a theological testimony about activities within the faith community. This theological testimony brings with it the responsibility to reflect as rightly as possible on the character of God by demonstrating the sort of virtue and character aligned with the collective call of God's people from darkness to light. In offering such testimony, Christian reporters do so as members of the community of faith and, thus, must speak as members of the body trained up to offer appropriate theological testimony. Journalists and bloggers like all other members of the church must learn to speak the language of the church, which "is the community that speaks Chrsitianese, and theology formulates the syntax and semantics of this language."[171]

Christian authors are responsible for the sort of truth-telling that corresponds to the reality of God with us. Such truth-telling need not preclude reports concerning the missteps or misdeeds of individual Christians or Christian organizations, as long as such reports contribute to a transformative discourse.[172] In *Beyond News*, Stephens calls for what he refers to as "wisdom journalism," which, among other things, "does not withhold opinion, but it should be opinion that not only is fair to other points of view but has been tested and strengthened by exposure to contrary opinion."[173] Stephens describes a sort of journalism that does not "lead an audience 'into anger'," but inspires ongoing dialogue and engagement with (not violence against) those who hold opposing viewpoints. Reporting will almost certainly entail interpretation and opinion, but it should also recognize uncertainty and acknowledge the validity of other perspectives.

Christian authors seeking to expose or otherwise address present-day crises and scandals would do well to consider how such public reporting conveys God to the world, as well as the sort of dialogue such reporting encourages.[174] In one sense, the impact of a particular author's words (a) cannot be predicted and (b) are not the sole responsibility of the author. In another sense, author's must learn to anticipate the sort of response a given work may elicit, as well as making an effort not to encourage polarized reactions by suppressing counter-narratives or by offering selective accounts of events filled with unfounded accusations or uninformed (or under-informed) perspectives.[175]

The impact on the communal witness, as well as the manner in which such reporting shapes Christian discourse cannot be ignored. To the extent that Christian authors promote disunity and discord, they must take on that responsibility and discern, as members of the church, whether using the "power of the pen" to broadcast scandals represents faithful, public Christian testimony. Certainly men and women who engage in inappropriate behavior that harms the body of Christ should be held accountable. Yet the quest for accountability or "justice" within the church is not an authorization to use any means necessary to bring deviant members to heel.[176] Those who report such events bear the burden of responsibility for their actions as well.

Such considerations are not simply left to the discernment of an isolated, independent author. The discernment of Christian authors must be shaped by the broader Christian "mind" that has been cultivated by the community of faith. As Hauerwas rightly states regarding theological writing, "The ability to write well theologically relies on a church to exist that makes such writing possible."[177] So, while Christian authors are certainly responsible for the public testimony they offer, they are not alone in this responsibility. The body of Christ is responsible for the sort of discourse that occurs within the church in the digital age or any other. Responsible theological testimony requires responsible Christian authors *and* a responsible Christian community. It is to this latter requirement that we will now turn.

Responsible Christian Community

While it is certainly appropriate for us to hold leaders responsible, we cannot ignore the fact that some monsters are of our own making. There is a reason that prominent pastors, leaders, or other personalities are prominent…we as a community see characteristics in them that we feel exemplify certain significant ideals that we value in our community. Prominent Christians, those who serve as a "voice" and "face" of the Christian community or some aspect of it, are not self-made women and men. Our donations support their radio programs or websites, our dollars demonstrate to publishers that we have an interest in reading their thoughts, our attendance at their conferences give the impression that we want to hear them speak, and the list goes on.

Holding up women and men who exemplify our community ideals is not fundamentally problematic, nor is it particularly avoidable. The development of prototypes which "describe individual cognitive representations of group norms" is part of mapping the boundaries of a group.[178] If this sort of prototyping is a common part of the process of group definition, then the problem may not be with the establishment of prototypes *per se*, but with the identification of the key characteristics or "fuzzy sets, not checklists, of attributes (e.g., attitudes and behaviors)" used to "define one group and distinguish it from other groups."[179]

In other words, perhaps the problem is that we are rallying around a set of attitudes and behaviors too limited to account for the sorts of characteristics we ought to be identifying as prototypical of the Christian community. Perhaps we are contributing to the bad behaviors of certain members of our community by too narrowly focusing on an incomplete set of valued attitudes and behaviors.[180] Perhaps our leaders are not solely a product of their own moral failure or lack of wisdom…perhaps they are also a product of our own misunderstanding of who we are as a community.

When we select a leader and allow that individual to "have disproportionate influence, through possession of consensual prestige or the exercise of power, or both, over the attitudes, behaviors, and destiny of group members," we affirm that this particular member reflects who we are as a community. This affirmation assumes that we know deeply our own group's norms and conventions and that such norms and conventions are sufficient to sustain the community in the midst of the challenges it faces. While it seems clear that we have a handle on some of the group norms (e.g. ability to preach the word with boldness, willingness to speak truth to power, etc.), there is a need for this aspect of group identity to be an ongoing site of negotiation.[181]

The community of faith as a social group is responsible for identifying those members who are afforded influence. It is also responsible for a given leader's deviance from specific communal norms. We collectively allow it to happen. As Abrams notes, "…both innovation and transgression by leaders may be enabled through psychological processes that create 'deviance credit,' which refers to group members' willingness to forego the obligations and social contracts of group membership and to give ingroup leaders the autonomy to diverge from group norms."[182]

Leaders do not have infinite credit and there are times when the community reacts against deviations from community norms. When it is perceived that a more limited set of attitudes and behaviors are challenged by aberrant belief or behavior (whether real or imagined), our community acts against the threat to preserve the social identity of the community *construed as essential*. Herein lies the challenge. If we understand ourselves to be, at our core, a community of justice and purity, we may react to ensure that justice and purity is maintained rather than focusing on restoration, forgiveness, and redemption which may be viewed as more ancillary to the community of faith.[183]

Dissonance within a group prompts similar group dynamics as one might expect in response to threats from outside of a group.[184] As Hogg and Reid note, "A schism effectively transforms one group, a single category, into two separate groups that are engaged in often highly charged intergroup conflict."[185] These conflicts are driven by perceived threats (real or imagined) to the social identity of the group. In Christian circles, such threats often boil down to theological positions not all of which are necessarily central to the gospel or to an orthodox stance. That "schisms can sometimes be very destructive of groups" seems obvious, yet there seems to be a willingness to split the group rather than evaluating the limits of the community or actually listening to one another long enough to realize that no social or (more importantly) biblical norm is being violated.[186]

Perceived threats to the community of faith encourage dynamics in which existing (negative) "attitudes and behavioural [sic] dispositions" toward different groups and members of the faith community deemed a threat to the community's social identity, "are exacerbated."[187] Perceived threats to the body of Christ underscore and heighten our awareness of the differences between the church and the world. At the same time, perceived threats foster tensions within the body of Christ producing a range of potential responses including marginalization or expulsion of certain "deviant" members of the group. On the other hand, Hogg and Martin note that the dynamics of prototyping "fairly automatically imbues the most prototypical member of a group with many attributes of leadership—for example, status, charisma, popular support, and the ability to influence."[188] Both the marginalization of deviant group members and the authorization of group members who appear to be "most prototypical" demonstrate the importance of the "sets of attitudes and behaviors" the body of Christ decides to treat as normative…as prototypical.

As this exploration of group dynamics suggests, the community of faith is not without responsibility when a given leader goes "off the rails," nor is the community of faith without responsibility when Christian authors are allowed to become influencers with "disproportionate power and influence to set agenda, define identity, and mobilize people to achieve collective goals."[189] We collectively own the damage done by those we authorize as influencers. We collectively own the malformation of believers who find it appropriate to malign fellow members of the body in public on the basis of little to no evidence. We collectively own Christian discourse that does not engage in constructive dialogue, but demeans, polarizes, and marginalizes members of the body. Perhaps worst, we collectively own the portrayal of God as one for whom seemingly any means are justified by the accomplished ends.

If we have forgotten that we are to be a community characterized as being poor in spirit, mournful, meek, hungry and thirsty for righteousness, merciful, pure in heart, seekers of peace, persecuted for righteousness, and reviled for Christ, we have lost an important sense of who we are in Christ.[190] If we have forgotten that we are to be a community capable of recognizing who belongs to us and who doesn't, we will surely lose our way. But if we determine to become a community who is so consumed with purity that we neglect unity through the dismissal of difference, we will have lost the unique, mysterious character that makes the body of Christ so compelling.

The responsible Christian community recognizes that the body of Christ has boundaries and limits. There are certainly beliefs and behaviors that cannot go unchecked by the community of faith. At the same time, the community of faith recognizes that the way in which deviant beliefs and behaviors are addressed must also be in line with the character of the body of Christ. This latter recognition must call into question the reporting of public allegations which, true or not, create fissures in the community of faith, distract the community from its core work of proclaiming the gospel, and, particularly in the digital age in which we live, promotes one-sided (often polarizing) discourse that never goes away.[191]

Media, Accountability, and Public Christian Testimony

It seems clear that authors and the community of which they are part have a responsibility to offer faithful Christian testimony in the public sphere. It is certainly appropriate for those who report on happenings within the body of Christ to report on both positive and negative events. It is tempting, at this point, to default to a call for "fair and balanced" reporting, but "fair and balanced" may, at times, run counter to the deeper values of the Christian community. Surely, Christians must demand reports that honor the individuals involved through a particular sort of description. At the most basic level, however, the body of Christ must demand theologically faithful accounts. It is this criteria that must serve as the standard for all public Christian testimony.

A theologically faithful account is not one that ignores the tensions and problems that exist within the body of Christ. Such an account would not gloss over the shortcomings and sins of the body. The scriptures themselves contain theological accounts revealing the failings of God's people as in (1) David's abuse of power in his liaison with Bathsheba and conspiracy to murder Uriah, (2) Israel's rejection of God's order in their refusal to keep Sabbath, (3) Peter's three-fold denial of Christ, or (4) the church's struggles to remain faithful in the midst of a fallen world. While this paradigm may appear to authorize the modern-day practice of reporting on the failings of leaders and institutions publicly in order to encourage, if not force, change and repentance, there are at least three factors that should give modern-day authors pause before claiming to be in line with this biblical trajectory.

First, the Bible is an inspired document written to reveal God. The authors of Scripture and the prophets whose oracles are recorded therein represent the infallible word of God. They aren't based solely on human report or observation, nor are they clouded by the sort of agendas and biases that human writers working outside of an inspired text might bring. The Bible is the definition of a theologically faithful account. It was revealed by God to point those who read it to Him. Modern-day reports cannot claim (nor do I assume they would) similar revelatory status. As such, modern-day reporters must leave open the possibility that their observations are partial and their interpretations limited.

Second, the biblical authors recorded the events they did for a particular purpose across a range of genres. Each of these genres "coordinates three related aspects of communicative action: the enactment of the author's intent, the engagement with the world, and the encounter with the addressee."[192] The biblical genres are adapted to convey a theological reality within a broader discourse context. Genres structure discrete moments of communication, but they also "…accumulate forms of seeing and interpreting particular aspects of the world."[193] Given this latter function of genre, modern-day communicators cannot afford to be naïve in the adoption of any genre (including that of theological essay).

Adapting a modern-day genre so that it does not simply conform to the commonplace conventions, but conveys a perspective of the world that recognizes God's activity in and position over the world seems a task appropriate to modern-day Christian communicators. Do we understand the nature of a theologically faithful tweet? Can we convey a theologically faithful account of reality through our Instagram or Facebook posts?[194] How is it that a web-based report or blog renders reality so as to demonstrate the character of God?

That the biblical authors (and Author) wrote with the particular purpose of revealing God as He intersects with the world. Whether it be in narrative, poetry, epistle, or proverb, God shows Himself within the realm of lived human experience. As such, the reports of human failings are a bit more than coincidental, but not much more than coincidental. The failure of David with Bathsheba was not a critique of kingship, but a reminder that Israel's hope could not be with David. Even the Lord's anointed is still the Lord's and is a poor substitute for God Himself. We cannot look to the scriptures for a justification to venerate or scandalize our leaders. We can look to them as a paradigm for telling the story of God in the world.

Finally, the differences in interactivity within the modern-day media culture must also be taken into consideration. We do communicate with the intention of impacting those with whom we communicate. We may even want those with whom we communicate to communicate back in some way. However, some forms of communication seem less conducive to mass media interactions, particularly real-time interactions. Authors who post on social media must attend to more than their own writing…they must begin to anticipate the reactions of those to whom they are communicating.

When we publish opinions and perspectives without sufficient grounding in fact, question the motives or wisdom of others, or convey unfounded accusations, we do so knowing that what we publish may spread (and often hoping it will spread quickly). The negative portrayals of God's people in the scriptures are, among other things, intended to reinforce a theological reality. They are not news items intended to create political pressure, rally support for a particular perspective, or convey information to the broader body of Christ so that they may form their own opinions and perspectives.[195] If, as Stephens argues, "wisdom journalism" is of the sort "that strengthens our understanding of the world," how much more should Christian journalism and reporting strengthen our understanding of God and set forth a theological account of the body of Christ.[196]

As certain individual Christians have gained prominence, we as a community have given ourselves over to be influenced by their teachings and to support their ministries often in an uncritical and unreflective manner. Such teaching is abstracted from the concrete challenges of our local community. We lean in to listen to women and men who have developed large followings which constructs a façade of success and stability. The teaching has been attached to a "hyperreal" persona that portrays a substance of character when there may actually be none.[197]

We who listen and watch from afar are in a less-than-optimal position to assess the Christian character of those who write the books we read, preach on the programs to which we listen or subscribe, or produce our favorite podcast. We trust that a local body of believers is holding accountable those who speak to us through mass media or run a national or international ministry. When that local body doesn't hold their most prominent members accountable, we, as a broader community, have embraced and encouraged those who shed light on the dark deeds of prominent individuals or institutions to act in the stead of a local body.

This practice, however, seems problematic because abstracting accountability from within the context of a particular local body of Christ disempowers those within the local body.[198] In part, this disempowerment is related to the manner in which social media reports, or even reports from more traditional journalistic sources, heavily influence the course of conversations by demanding answers to questions that may or may not be of any consequence. This influence makes the local community…the people with the highest stakes…subject to outside forces which react to partial information and may be lacking perspective about the true challenges facing the community and how to fix them. Surely outside pressure can play a role. Some conversations might never occur were it not for media reports that force the hand of a particular leader or group of leaders. But, just because mass media accountability has a positive impact, doesn't make it an appropriate or even a particularly effective means for achieving the end of a more unified, faithful body of Christ.[199]

When reports determine the topics of discussion, they exert a particular sort of power over a situation for which they have no particular responsibility to fix. In the worst case scenario, the public relations machine and legal apparatus (which often provide a different sort of questionable framing) begin the damage control process. Meanwhile, leadership seeks to address accusations in a manner that will, as much as possible, sustain the status quo while silencing critics. Though this description of the dynamics associated with a "social firestorm" may be an over-generalization, it is intended as a heuristic to underscore Gladwell's point about networks: "The drawbacks of networks scarcely matter if the network isn't interested in systemic change—if it just wants to frighten or humiliate or make a splash—or if it doesn't need to think strategically."[200] He goes on to note, "The instruments of social media are well suited to making the existing social order more efficient. They are not a natural enemy of the status quo."[201]

In one of the better case scenarios the frustration expressed through networked efforts will drive superficial change. In the worst case, organizations and their networked critics reinforce one another, particularly when critics depend on increasing and/or maintaining an audience to retain influence. Critics are able to appear bold in their stance against "the establishment" while organizations are able to do some innocuous pruning and continue relatively unscathed into the future...with no real systemic change.

Conclusion

We live in a moment in which more authors are able to speak more often with fewer personal and professional filters. We also live in a moment in which readers are encouraged to participate in online conversations and to express their opinions (informed or otherwise). The digital environment in which we find ourselves is one in which vast amounts of information are available to us though we may seldom push ourselves to read authors that challenge rather than reinforce our existing perspectives. The tendency toward more surface-level interaction with a topic seems almost inevitable given the sheer volume of information to which we have access and with which we are bombarded through email, text, and alerts from our favorite sites or apps. There is less and less time, it would seem, to think deeply and reflectively about a situation, to do research, or to check our sources...it is far simpler to form a coherent story based on the information we have available and run with it.

Beyond the volume of information, we are also living in an era of easy participation in which joining an "online firestorm" requires little to no effort...and has little to no effect. Change is not easy and requires more than a willingness to like, comment, or retweet. That means that the body of Christ must demand works that require us to expend mental energy rather than having our existing perspectives reinforced or being distracted from the difficult work of the gospel by the scandal of the day.[202]

The body of Christ, if it is to be a community that gets beyond superficial issues to address whatever deeper dynamics may plague the Christian community, will need to consider what it is consuming and how what is consumed is impacting the communities of which we are a part. While it would be easy to place the full weight of responsibility on individual authors or speakers, the community of faith and every member of it bears the responsibility for ensuring that the public testimony of Christian writers and speakers reflects the sort of dialogue to which the body of Christ must aspire. Though our theological and doctoral positions are crucial, our community is not simply defined by the theological positions we hold. Equally crucial is the manner in which we demonstrate our love for one another.

7 Christians And Power

Introduction

Christians have (or at least have the opportunity to develop) a unique, theologically informed perspective on the world. The scriptures and the testimony of the church demonstrate that the normal and natural "state of things" is not set in stone. We need not resign ourselves to live in a world without hope for imminent change and ultimate transformation. God breaks into our settled world alerting those with eyes to see and ears to hear of his presence. Our unique view of the world results in "foolish" practices like prayer, fasting, Sabbath, and hospitality. Displaying the wisdom of God by engaging in wise practices…practices that appear foolish to the world…makes Christians strange. Yet, as strange as Christians may be, we are seldom strange enough, or, perhaps, not strange in the right ways.

We run the risk of accepting the current state of things as "natural" and adopting the logic of the age as our own. It is not so much that we need to be wholly separate from the world. We bring our particular identities with us into the body of Christ and, rather than eliminating any trace of those identities, our task is to ensure that our identity in Christ governs the others. Doing so requires that we develop a robust Christian identity allowing our potential for a unique, theologically informed vision to be realized individually and corporately.

Yet, we must also understand that we live in a world bent on assimilating us…fooling us into thinking that its ways and means are inevitable, non-negotiable, and necessary. For instance, in *To Change the World*, Hunter suggests,

> "…the state has increasingly become the incarnation of the public weal. Its laws, policies, and procedures have become the predominant framework by which we understand collective life, its members, its leading organizations, its problems and its issues…This is the heart of politicization and it has gone so far as to affect our language, imagination, and expectations. The language of politics (and political economy) comes to frame progressively more of our understanding of our common life, our public purposes, and ourselves individually and collectively."[203]

Hunter's account highlights the manner in which the operations of the state, particularly the democratic state, have influenced Christian movements from the Christian Right to the Christian Left and everything in-between (e.g. the Neo-Anabaptists). His concern is not that the workings of these various groups are somehow morally corrupt, but that in depending on and utilizing the power of the state "Christians have not been formed 'in all wisdom' that they might rise to the demands of faithfulness in a time such as ours, 'bearing fruit in every good work.'"[204]

Fitch, building on Hunter's work, notes the need for a different sort of individual and corporate Christian formation that will allow Christians to respond to Hunter's call for faithful presence. Fitch's concern is that the church will send men and women out to "be a faithful presence in their jobs, vocations, and spheres of influence" without being properly equipped to stand as Christians, thus increasing the odds that they will be assimilated into the world. Without churches sufficient to sustain a collective distinction and to form individual women and men of distinction, "The power structures of this world are not challenged. In the process the reality of church community as a social reality witnessing to God's kingdom in the world gets put aside. As a result the world will not be changed, but once again Christians will be."[205]

Hunter and Fitch both recognize that part of the challenge of Christian participation in the world involves Christian participation in the structures and logics of the world in a way that honors and preserves the distinctly Christian character of the community of faith. They are not calling the church to separate from the world, but to embody in a profound manner the conviction that God stands with the body of Christ and that, as such, the body of Christ cannot be broken. It is the conviction that the body and its individual members are "not sustained by bread alone, but on every word that comes from the mouth of God" (Deuteronomy 8:3). The body of Christ need not follow paths accepted by the world toward money, reputation, credibility, or power. We are "not sustained by bread alone," but on the promises of God as we live in accordance with his wisdom.

It is easy to say that we are to live strangely in the world…it is not easy to do. Navigating the complex landscape of the digital age, attempting to hold accountable leaders and institutions that transcend the limits of local geography through mass media, seeking to contribute our unique, individual perspectives, or just trying to sort out the barrage of information that comes at us in any given moment is no simple task. In addition to a myriad of other changes, our newly developed capacity for social sharing and networking has influenced the development of new opportunities and values in relation to power. While "old power" continues to exert a great deal of force, "new power" is, according to some accounts, making headway.[206]

Regardless of the forms of power available, the question remains as to what a theologically faithful appropriation and use of power might look like. Of course, we already have pictures that offer us insight into appropriate use of power in Christ's self-giving. Jesus's voluntary giving over of power in which He fully surrenders Himself for humanity by trusting the Father is instructive. In seeking to accomplish justice, there are certainly moments in Jesus's earthly ministry when he engages in public confrontation (cf. Matt 12:33-37; Mk 7:1-13); however, the kingdom was never to be ushered in through rhetorical genius, political savvy, or military might. Instead, true power was found in selfless service (Phil 2:4-7) and an unwavering commitment to God's will regardless of the consequences (2:8).

What might it mean for us to "..look not only to his own interests, but also to the interests of others" within the context of social media? How might we exercise appropriate voice and restraint as we seek to speak the truth in love while embodying the sort of self-surrender and trust in the Father that might appear to leave justice undone? When Christ died on the cross, it seems possible that some, even those who followed him, may have understood him as just another in a line of messianic pretenders. Yet, it was his act of willing sacrifice that, after his resurrection, would be seen as a victory over sin and death. It is for us to learn what it means to "Of particular interest is the Christian use of words in the context of a digital age in which using words is cheap, easy, and influential. Christians have an opportunity to model a different orientation to discourse in which the depth of discussion is only matched by the grace and respect shown to those who participate in it.

Power, Old and New

Before exploring what it might look like for Christians to use power in a theologically faithful manner, it will be important to offer at least a preliminary understanding of power. As a topic, power is a challenging concept to pin down with absolute certainty. In part, that is due to its adaptive nature so that "when we use the concept [of power] in different contexts its meaning changes sufficiently so that there is no single definition of power."[207] While power is difficult to define, there are some characteristics that are generally associated with it. Power, for instance, is generally recognized as ubiquitous, or ever-present. Most treatments of power also acknowledge power's influential effects and capacity to bring about change. Still, despite a general agreement about certain characteristics of power, the concept is far from uniform.

Russell, for instance, opts for a rather simple definition of power suggesting that it may be understood "as the production of intended effects" and that power is "a quantitative concept."[208] Power is, for Russell, the "fundamental concept in social science" such that attempting to study "one form of power, say wealth, in isolation, can only be partially successful."[209] He goes on to suggest that "inequality in the distribution of power has always existed in human communities, as far back as our knowledge extends," attributing the unequal distribution, in part, to "external necessity" and, in part, to "human nature."[210] Russell sees power as an ever-present factor in human relations which makes both positive and negative contributions to the lives of individuals and groups.

Arendt offers a slightly different understanding of power which is created when individuals act together to initiate some new endeavor in contrast to individual acts that may build strength, which is different than power. Strength, in Arendt's view, may increase apart from power as in the case of escapism. Arendt does not describe escapism in wholly negative terms, but acknowledges that "flight from the world in dark times of impotence can always be justified as long as reality is not ignored, but is constantly acknowledged as the thing that must be escaped…it is essential for them to realize that the realness of this reality consists not in its deeply personal note…but inheres in the world from which they have escaped."[211] Strength and power, however, are not "the same" and, perhaps not even positively correlated in Arendt's thought. Instead, finding its origins in collective action, power trumps strength, which is more fundamentally individual.

In *On Violence*, Arendt contrasts power and violence noting, "politically speaking, it is insufficient to say that power and violence are not the same. Power and violence are opposites; where the one rules absolutely, the other is absent."[212] This perspective allows for a clear separation of power and violence so that "Violence appears where power is in jeopardy, but left to its own course ends in power's disappearance."[213] Power has a more positive, collective character in which individuals join together to accomplish some end.

Fairclough offers yet another perspective on power. Concerning power, Fairclough notes, "one aspect of power is the capacity to impose and maintain a particular structuring of some domain or other—a particular way of dividing it into parts, of keeping the parts demarcated from each other, and a particular ordering of those parts in terms of hierarchical relations of domination and subordination."[214] Power for Fairclough shapes the social worlds in which we exist, in part, through language.

In this way, Fairclough's understanding resonates with Bourdieu's treatments of symbolic power which is involves an authoritative structuring of the social world rather than being forcefully imposed. Symbolic power is the fruit of symbolic violence, which is "a gentle violence, imperceptible and invisible even to its victims, exerted for the most part through the purely symbolic channels of communication and cognition (more precisely, misrecognition), recognition, or even feeling."[215] Power, or symbolic power in Bourdieu's thought, is fundamentally a means by which certain individuals or institutions exercise subtle, often unnoticed, dominance.

Taking a still different approach, Heimans and Timms suggest that power may be exercised "on a vastly greater scale and with greater potential impact than we did even a few years ago."[216] They go on to note that our fundamental behaviors and expectations have shifted as the technological environment has dramatically changed. These changes have created a context in which we must learn "to navigate and thrive in a world defined by the battle and balancing of two big forces…old power and new power."[217] According to Heimans and Timms, "Old power is like a currency. It is held by a few…jealously guarded, and the powerful have a substantial store of it to spend. It is closed inaccessible, and leader-driven. It downloads, and it captures."[218] By contrast, new power "is like a current…made by many…open, participatory, and peer-driven. It uploads, and it distributes…it's forceful when it surges. The goal with new power is not to hoard it but to channel it."[219]

For Heimans and Timms, the differences between new power and old power are rooted in the values underlying these two sorts of power. Old Power privileges formal governance, competition, discretion, specialization, and long-term loyalty with less participation. New power has a more informal governance, utilizes crowd wisdom and collaboration, practices radical transparency, has a maker culture, and requires more of a short-term conditional affiliation.[220] These new power values create a context in which networked groups of committed individuals pooling resources (monetary or otherwise) working together toward a common, if short-term, goal can wreak havoc on larger established organizations. New power groups understand the power they wield and refuse to be consumers…passive individuals and groups to whom a company sells goods or services of value. Instead, new power groups desire to participate in the company rather than simply consuming a product.

New power groups are stakeholders. They are not buyers, but partners in the businesses and movements in which they choose to affiliate. They recognize the interdependent nature of the relationship between a customer or user base and press the companies with whom they interact to do the same. For example, in 2016, qgyh2, a Reddit account holder, offered an insight that exemplifies the move toward new power: "Reddit, when your investors sit in their special cave and count their money they list reddit.com as their main asset here. Reddit.com is not your main asset. Reddit's users and community are your main asset. If you treat them badly you will lose them."[221]

Despite its "newness," new power and the accompanying values noted by Heimans and Timms share more with old power than might be readily evident in their analysis. Both new and old power operate based on coordinated action. While old power may well have been exercised through what Naim refers to as the "Weberian bureaucratic ideal," new power requires organizing principles in order to mobilize a base sufficient to warrant notice.[222] Though it is certainly the case that the organization involved with new power is looser and less formal than the "Weberian bureaucracy," the dynamics involved in exercising new power still require the consolidation of a set of wills greater than the consolidation of other wills in order to maintain a particular status quo or effect a specific change. In other words, there continues to be a struggle for "the capacity to impose a particular social vision of the world as the most legitimate one."[223] The fundamental direction of power has not changed even if the values underlying the use of power have.

Naim describes the rise of certain new power dynamics in his discussion of "micropowers," which are now in a position to challenge "megaplayers." Micropowers employ a different sort of power that is "…not the massive, overwhelming, and often coercive power of large and expert organizations but the counterpower that comes from being able to oppose and constrain what those big players can do."[224] These micropowers, according to Naim, "wear down, impede, undermine, sabotage, and outflank the megaplayers."[225] Naim does not see the disruption of megaplayers as wholly positive or without potentially negative side effects. Moving from the consolidation of power to a greater distribution of power may, according to Naim, "generate instability, disorder, and paralysis in the face of complex problems."[226]

The shifts in power described in *The End of Power* and *New Power* have arisen, in part, as a reaction to the disappointment with existing institutions and leadership. We now find ourselves in a disruptive context with a seemingly never ending stream of ideas and opinions through which we must sift. Those who are capable of providing some semblance of a solution or promising a world free of at least some of our frustrations have ample opportunity to build an audience. They can find collaborators willing to believe that "radical transparency" and simple stories are more truthful than complex tales. They can cultivate crowd wisdom that might be more aptly characterized as a mob mentality whose opt-in decision-making is no less arbitrary or capricious than the CEO's strategic choices that are really motivated by a desire to see a rise in his or her stock portfolio. They can rally a critical mass of voices whose moral outrage and cheap participation is less a product of informed opinion than a knee-jerk reaction derived from fear, frustration, and anger.

We currently occupy an environment in which we are vulnerable to "terrible simplifiers," the "demagogues who seek power by exploiting the ire and frustration of the population and making appealing, but 'terribly simplified' and, ultimately, deceitful promises."[227] The instability in the environment creates a context in which "it has become far easier for newcomers—including those with toxic ideas—to acquire power."[228] As such, as the previously settled powers and structures of our world are questioned, we would be wise to be cautious of those who offer easy answers or those who reinforce our baser instincts as they tell tales devoid of God and, thus, devoid of hope.

Working with Power Tools (and Keeping All Your Fingers)

Wielding the technologies of the digital world provides new opportunities for new voices to take advantage of new power values. They can advance agendas outside of "Weberian bureaucracies," and disrupt established systems. These new opportunities are not all bad…or all good. The question is whether Christians who wield this new power are willing and able to do so in ways that demonstrate a commitment to promoting unity in the body of Christ and offering faithful public testimony. It will be up to those who wield power of any sort to do so in a manner that seeks to reform the identity of the body of Christ. We need them to use new power to cultivate new dispositions and a new *habitus* sustained by new communal norms and values more adequate to a body subject to God's authority.[229] If, instead, we use our new opportunities to reinforce current power dynamics or simply to put those on the bottom at the top and those on top at the bottom, we will not have accomplished the sort of radical transformation called for by the gospel.

Christians who exercise new power will ultimately face the same fundamental challenges as those who exercise(d) old power; that is, wielding that power in a manner that honors God, proclaims the gospel, and strengthens and reinforces the body of Christ. Wielding power in this manner requires more than an ethical commitment to "do no harm." It requires an ongoing submission to God's authority so that the exercise of power shapes the body of Christ in such a way that the church conforms ever more closely to the image of Christ. Similarly, to wield power faithfully will involve both risk and restraint if we are to recognize that we exercise power under the authority of God. Our role is not to save the world, but to offer faithful testimony in thought, word, and deed…to participate as a member of the body in such a way that we contribute to the church's recognition that it needs to be the church.

Such submission is a matter of individual, not isolated, Christian practice. Power, to the extent that any given individual wields it, is exercised within a broader set of relationships some of which are relatively straightforward and others which are more complex. Individual Christian practice recognizes and embraces the relational quality of life rather than retreating into a deluded isolationism in which our responsibility to and love for other members of the the body is made less-than necessary.

Individual Christian practice always has an impact (positive or negative) on others. Each of us is individually positioned to have a unique impact on the body of Christ and its members. Individual Christian practice does not take place in a vacuum. It occurs within a "dialectical" context in which individuals and institutions act upon one another, so that "individuals…are constitutive of a social order and its institutions. But at the same time, those institutions and the larger social order of which they are a part not only provide the framework of meanings and social relations in which individuals operate but also 'act back' on individuals to form the structures of their consciousness."[230]

Though individuals and institutions impact one another "…in the formation of culture, one should not be under the illusion that the dialectic is evenly balanced. While individuals are not powerless by any stretch of the imagination, institutions have much greater power."[231] In essence, our individual Christian practice may, and perhaps in many cases should, oppose the institutions that "act back" on us as individual image-bearers and as members of the unified body of Christ. We may well find ourselves in a state of constant opposition to a myriad of forces with the power to divide the body of Christ, distort the image of Christ we convey, and/or subsume our identity in Christ beneath labels like "evangelical," "conservative," or "American."[232]

This dialectic between individual and institution is prominent in discussions of what is often referred to as "whiteness." According to Carter,

> "…whiteness names the activation of a certain set of dispositions. These dispositions cover the full panoply of reality. Thus, the activation of these dispositions creates the scholar (in this case, the historian), and, then once

created, these same dispositions name the conditions under which the scholar is habituated (*habitus*). The traditional construal of reality such that historians have been unable or unwilling to renarrate the story of America so as to make sense of black existence—and the existence of others as well—reflects the degree to which historians have activated and lived into the dispositions of the academic. Thus, to be a historian is to activate that set of dispositions that enables a certain form of storytelling while disabling others."[233]

Such dynamics are not limited to matters of color or race, but are deeply embedded in the relationships between classes and genders. Speaking of his experience as a young, lower-middle class scholarship student attending an exclusive New England prep school, Hedges notes,

"I spent time in the mansions of the ultra-rich and powerful, watching my classmates, who were children, callously order around men and women who worked as their chauffeurs, cooks, nannies, and servants…The rich have a disdain for the poor—despite carefully publicized acts of philanthropy—and a haughty dislike of the middle class."[234]

These dispositions, whether related to race, class, or some other arbitrary standard supported by the various economic, cultural, and symbolic capitals that have been deemed to "matter," are propagated through established systems that have a monopoly on a particular form of currency.

In his introduction to *The Pursuit of Happiness and Other Sobering Thoughts*, George Will offers an insight on institutions, particularly the institution of the state noting, "Men and women are biological facts. Ladies and gentlemen—citizens—are social artifacts, works of political art. They carry the culture that is sustained by wise laws and traditions of civility. At the end of the day we are right to judge society by the character of the people it produces. That is why statecraft is, inevitably, soulcraft."[235] The language of "social artifacts" is not limited to the activity of the state, however influential it may be, but may be extended to include any institution in which one may accumulate symbolic capital "in the form of knowledge, technical know-how, credentials, and cultural accomplishments."[236]

We are, in many ways, formed and shaped by our devotion to the pursuit of "capital." As a concept, "capital" is not limited to money, but may be broadened to include any "possession" or cultivated characteristic or skill that gives one more credibility than others within a given context. In academia, it might be the number of peer-reviewed articles one has published. In the world of art, "taste" becomes a rather subjective form of capital. Increasingly, victimization or alignment with victims is becoming a means of gaining social cache. In the evangelical church, popularity and ability to grow a ministry seems to become a sort of sign of God's blessing…unless of course you are Joel Osteen.

For Christians, we must remember that it is not possible to "serve God and money" (Matt 6:24), nor is it possible to serve God and any other form of capital that distracts us from our pursuit of "the kingdom of God and his righteousness" (Matt 6:33). Our individual Christian practice…our faithful presence in the world…cannot be fueled by anxiety over or desire for the various forms of earthly capital, but by our individual and collective commitment to "the kingdom of God and his righteousness."[237] Rather than accumulating some arbitrary form of capital that may be used to exert our will on others, within the church we must begin to learn how to allow individuals to earn respect through wise living as determined by the instruction of God carried through the community of faith. As O'Donovan notes, "It is not as bearer of his own primitive pre-social or pre-political rights that the individual demands the respect of the community, but as the bearer of a social understanding which recalls the formative self-understanding of the community itself."[238]

Power and Language- Some Underlying Assumptions

The relationship between power and language is complex and varied particularly after the so-called postmodern turn. Themes of power and oppression intermingle with concerns related to epistemology and meaning making.[239] As interesting and pertinent as a review of this literature might be, the following offers only an abbreviated treatment of the field with the intention of teasing out some implications for those who engage in discourse through digital media in a digital age. This brief summary makes a few key assumptions concerning the relationship between power and language use that need to be made explicit.

First, the existence of power dynamics within the use of language does not necessarily entail an oppressor/oppressed relationship. While it is certainly true that oppressors may co-opt language for nefarious ends, oppression is not inherent in language use.[240] Discussion and dialogue between parties involves a more fluid ceding of power between individuals. Though it is certainly the case that language and language use reflect underlying social imaginaries, it is not the case that anytime someone with more power or privilege speaks they are oppressing another, nor is it the case that language always encodes oppressive mechanisms into its fundamental structure.

Oppression, when understood in the sense of the active denial of equal opportunity, is not inherent in language alone.[241] Language may play a role, but it is not the only actor on the stage. Even so, language and language use can and do contribute to the reinforcement of particular social imaginaries. As such, oppression may be understood to occur to the extent that a social imaginary and the language used to express it denies God, distorts His character, or functions so as to pervert the order he has put in place by imposing on those who bear His image an order apart from God.

From the perspective of the Christian mind, the presence of a hierarchy is not the central problem, but inappropriate power relations within a hierarchy. Such relations begin with the rejection of God's sovereign authority to order the world and, by extension, to determine the manner in which we understand it and speak about it. Language that is oppressive is also fundamentally un-Christian. The development of a full theology of hierarchy and power is beyond the scope of the current essay. It should be noted that the characteristics of a Christian mind account for several fundamental issues associated with power, hierarchy and oppression, including, but not necessarily limited to: (1) the incomplete nature of human perspectives, (2) the rejection of systems and structures that curtail Christian imagination and progressive conformity to Christ, (3) the demand for accountability, and (4) the transient nature of systems and institutions. Social imaginaries, even those informed by theology, are not sacrosanct or inevitable, but provisional, flawed attempts to order social arrangements in a world for which disorder has been embedded.

So, for better or worse, language reinforces underlying social imaginaries. In part, this function of language is the primary reason that words have such power. To the extent that our descriptions of the world structure or reinforce the way we relate within it, language has the potential for misuse and abuse. Language, however, is not inherently oppressive…it can also be liberating. Take, for instance, the sentence, "Jesus is Lord." While many would see such language as exclusive and narrow-minded, "Jesus is Lord" is both an expression of allegiance and freedom. It is not oppressive, but articulates God's reign (a hierarchy with God at the top) and calls for a particular relation to God (one of faithful obedience).

Second, the labels of "oppressed" and "oppressors" cannot be applied simply based on social position. The Bible is not silent regarding the issue of oppression. While the language is most often used in terms of the domination of one nation over another (Exod 3:9; 22:21; Judges 1:34; 2:18; 4:3; 6:9; 10:12; 1 Sam 10:18; 2 Kings 13:4, 22; Psalms 56:1; 106:42; Isa 19:20; Jer 30:20; Amos 6:14), it is also found in contexts concerning the treatment of sojourners (Exod 23:9). The basic biblical understanding of the term appears to be less related to position or hierarchy and more to a mentality of dominance in which the dominated, or oppressed, group is treated as a resource to be exploited or object to be controlled and, perhaps, eventually weeded out of society.

More to the point is the perversion of God's order that is necessarily associated with oppression. Oppression functionally denies God his position as Sovereign, as well as denying the God-given position of the oppressed. Oppression occurs when one group actively (often coercively) seeks to displace or otherwise control the destiny of another, thus taking on the mantle of God.[242] The biblical account does not appear to call for radical equality or the elimination of hierarchy. Instead, the Bible appears to identify oppression as a particular form of overreaching whereby the social fabric of reality is misdetermined by one group's exercise of power over another. This overreaching normally results in some sort of denial of God or a co-opting of God into one's own personal agenda. In this sense, oppression is a fundamentally theological problem that may be exacerbated or conditioned by position because of its basic usurping of God's authority to order creation and the creatures within it.

Third, it is not as if the impulse to determine the destiny of others…to take on the role of God…is limited to struggles between groups. Oppression within groups does not somehow excuse the oppression of one group by another. Rather, it forces us to look beyond our "normal" revolutionary affinities and our tendencies for justice. Rearranging the hierarchy or eliminating one group of oppressors may be part of the solution, but it cannot solve the problem.

We must recognize that once again Christ is the solution to oppression. In Philippians 2, Paul calls the church in Philippi to a lifestyle that does not seek one's own well being at the expense of others: "Do nothing from selfish ambition or conceit, but in humility count others more significant than yourselves. Let each of you look not only to his own interests, but also to the interests of others" (Phil 2:3-4). This lifestyle is exemplified by Christ. Christ, being equal with God, did not see equality with God as something to be held to Himself. Being God entailed self-giving rather than aloof detachment unwilling to get one's hands dirty. As such, Christ became human and humbled himself by obeying the will of the Father (2:7-8). Christ's exaltation demonstrates that His humbling, sacrificial act and what was accomplished through it "was the outworking of the very character of God, the revelation of *divine* love."[243] It is this understanding of what it means to be equal with God that has implications for God's people. As Wright notes, "…as God endorsed Jesus' interpretation of what equality with God meant in practice, so he will recognize self-giving love in his people as the true mark of the life of the Spirit. Christ's own example is held up for the church to imitate; not that his incarnation, death and exaltation are *merely* exemplary, but they are *at least* that."[244]

In the formation of the Church, Christ brought together previously separate groups (e.g. Jews and Gentiles, men and women, slave and free, etc.) not for the purpose of obliterating the differences between them, but to demonstrate the fundamental reordering of social relations (and reality itself) driven by belief in the resurrected Christ. The body of Christ is a body in which each member is joined with and complements the other members under the authority of the body's head…the risen Christ. Hierarchies within the body of Christ exist in the sense that God has assigned certain members to certain tasks, given certain members more resources than others, and so on; however, such hierarchies must be understood as (1) existing under Christ's authority (1 Cor 11:3; Eph 1:22; 4:15; 5:23; Col 1:18; 2:10, 19), (2) utilized or not utilized for the building up of the body as a whole (Rom 1:11-12; 1 Cor 14:6-12; Eph 4:9-16; 6:1-9), and (3) being governed by the sort of impartiality (Deut 16:19; Acts 10:34; Eph 6:9; James 2:1, 9) fitting for a community whose origin flows from a common faith.

Finally, while the work on intersectionality is often associated with "identity politics" that would identify white, male, evangelicals as having "white privilege" and exercising power over those of a different race, gender, or ideology, intersectionality does offer some degree of clarity regarding the influence of group identities on the development of individuals. In her essay on intersectionality, Crenshaw describes the challenge of separating aspects of intersecting identities when approaching broad social issues: "Although racism and sexism readily intersect in the lives of real people, they seldom do in feminist and antiracist practices."[245] The basic idea of intersectionality is that there are a combination of factors and characteristics that influence one's experiences of the world. Race and gender have their place, but class, sexual orientation, religious affiliation, and a host of other factors also condition one's unique experience in the world.

As such, even those who are white and male can find points of empathy on the level of class, sexual orientation, religious affiliation or some other factor. It is not so much that the experience of a "white trash" male in rural America is the same as that of an impoverished African American female living in an urban slum, but that the sort of challenges "white trash" face in rural America are not wholly dissimilar from those faced by minorities living in an urban setting. Intersectionality has the potential to give those of us who have experienced the privileges of "whiteness" (at least some of them) an opportunity to tap into other parts of our identity which keep us from realizing the *full* privilege of being white.

The idea of partial privilege is illustrated well by Obermiller in his discussion of the migration of "hillbillies" to Detroit. While the hillbillies looked like native, white Detroiters, there were significant cultural and social differences that limited the hillbillies capacity to realize the same level of privilege as the native, white Detroiters despite being white. Obermiller observes:

> "For native, white Detroiters, the disturbing aspect of hillbillies was their racialness. Ostensibly, they were of the same racial order (whites) as those who dominated economic, political, and social power in local and national arenas. But hillbillies shared many regional characteristics with the southern blacks arriving in Detroit, which destabilized the fixity of northern racial stereotypes. The similarities and differences embodied by hillbillies indicate that markers of race and class had become conflated within this most salient rhetorical identity."[246]

What seems evident in this description is that being white is not, on its own, sufficient to realize all the privileges of being white.

Intersectionality is not without its challenges. Primary among them is its tendency to focus on individual characteristics that are not directly correlated with individual agency and responsibility. In other words, intersectionality is a "structural" concept that identifies the challenges faced by those who do not occupy the "privileged" mix of gender, class, ethnicity, religion, etc, rather than considering the role of behavior and choice to one's own achievement and well being. Recognizing the significance of the robust contribution of individual agency to one's individual success is as necessary as describing the complex social identities of individuals and the challenges associated with their varied combinations. Human beings exist as individuals with individual agency, but they do not do so in a vacuum. All of us are positively and negatively impacted by the systems and structures of the world. Individual achievement is not isolated achievement anymore than individual failure is isolated failure.

So, while it is easy to point to success stories of certain individuals from underprivileged backgrounds, the question of whether someone from such a background can succeed is not particularly helpful. Of course there are individuals from a variety of backgrounds that have achieved despite structural hinderances. A more revealing question might inquire as to the difference in effort, determination, focus, and "luck" necessary for someone from a less privileged position to succeed than might be needed for someone from a more privileged position. Similarly, one might ask to what extent a person from a more privileged position can retain stronger opportunities more easily (and perhaps while having less actual talent and character) due to the fact that they don't have to put forth as much effort, exercise as much determination, have as much focus, or get as "lucky" as someone from an less privileged position.

Power and Language

Having addressed some underlying assumptions and clarified an understanding of some key aspects of power, we can now further explore particular relations between power and language. In his brief essay entitled "Social Space and Symbolic Power," Pierre Bourdieu argues that social agents construct the world "under structural constraints." He suggests,

> "…the familiar world tends to be 'taken for granted,' perceived as natural. If the social world tends to be perceived as evident…this is because the dispositions of agents, their *habitus*, that is, the mental structures through which they apprehend the social world, are essentially the product of the internalization of the structures of that world."[247]

Human beings do not see the world in an unfiltered manner, but, often through a manufactured consent, agree to operate within the world under certain sets of assumptions and to pursue certain interests.[248] This agreement becomes the *de facto* understanding of "the way the world works." As such, they accept the state of things and act in accordance with the "natural" world. As Bourdieu notes, "…agents, even the most disadvantaged ones, tend to perceive the world as natural and to accept it much more readily than one might imagine…"[249]

Bourdieu connects the acceptance and construction of reality with language noting, "There is no social agent who does not aspire, as far as his circumstances permit, to have the power to name and to create the world through naming: gossip, slander, lies, insults, commendations, criticism, arguments and praises are all daily and petty manifestations of the solemn and collective acts of naming…"[250] The language of "aspire" suggests some sort of agenda for control, which likely overstates the case, since human beings often play a less-than intentional reinforcing role in the maintenance of existing "names." Such reinforcement is not always pernicious, but can occur for a whole range of motivations.

The aspect of Bourdieu's work that seems most significant at the moment is that we often act and interact with the world as if there is no alternative. Social agents participate in language and, many times, participate without a specific (or evil) agenda.[251] Language, regardless of the intention of any given social agent, is a means by which we develop frameworks for understanding the world around us and the various relationships in which we find ourselves. Whether the world is sustained "as is" or efforts are made to reform the status quo, language is an important tool.

The conditions in which language impacts our perspective on reality are not limited to those we might identify as maliciously manipulative such as is often associated with propaganda. Propaganda, while taking on a highly negative connotation post-World War II, "is not intrinsically evil or immoral," but is "a mode of mass persuasion, neither good nor evil, that can be enlisted for a variety of purposes and with a variety of results."[252] Propaganda's place of prominence in the strategies of the Nazi regime, has raised awareness of the dangers that propaganda may pose, as well as creating a derogatory connotation for a particular class of communication.

The ability to label a given communication as an instance of negative "propaganda" is not an altogether beneficial development as it can also mask the (negative?) force and (divisive?) function of propagated ideas that "circulate in public, reaching and drawing together large numbers of individuals who are largely unknown to one another."[253] Labeling something as "propaganda" can become a rhetorical technique designed to demonize and diminish a given position while vindicating or leaving unexamined other mass phenomena that may well have negative impact. Propaganda is "a central means of organizing and shaping thought and perception" delivered at scale requiring "institutions and media practices to take up the task of dissemination."[254] This way of understanding the term does not demand the negative connotation often attached to our normal use of "propaganda."

Social media has certainly changed the dynamics related to the propagation of information and the manner in which "the masses" are persuaded to a particular position. Though it may seem easiest to identify "fake news" as the most troublesome challenge facing the media world today, it would be a mistake to miss the broader unrest that conditions some people's ready acceptance of fake news. The broad suspicion of "official" reports and the emergence of new values and criteria for expertise have created a context when news need not be fake to create a feeding frenzy…it just needs to play on the too anxious psychology of the masses.[255]

New ways of speaking about the world are not limited to the content of speech (i.e. what is talked about). Rather, they include the modes of discourse utilized, the type of participation in such discourses, and the identification of those considered to be thought leaders who guide the discourse. The convergence of new technologies, distrust and/or disinterest in established voices, and a host of other factors have contributed to the popularization of new, often unlikely influencers who were, in part, in the right place at the right time. Peterson's comments on the Joe Rogan Experience express well this phenomenon:

> "…but fundamentally what has propelled you (Joe Rogan) to superstardom in some sense is not just your ability which is non-trivial but the fact that you're on this giant technological wave and you're one of the first adopters. And I'm in the same situation. We're first adopters of a technology that's as revolutionary as the Gutenberg printing press…the spoken word is now as powerful as the written word…and we're on the cutting edge of that for better or worse."[256]

Language and the ways in which it is employed have the ability to frame reality and to reorient or reinforce the manner in which we understand the various relations of our social world. As such, the manner in which Christians utilize language is inextricably intertwined with judgments related to our perception of the world and the relations within it. Language becomes a (if not the) key tool for describing a reality in which one action or set of actions are viewed as illegitimate, oppressive, or otherwise unfaithful and another action or set of actions are understood as necessary, noble, and righteous. Language…the way we describe God, ourselves, and our interactions with one another and the world…has the power to put us on level ground with God, to demonize our detractors, or to offer a complex treatment in which we recognize our limitations and acknowledge the contributions of others to our own understanding of the world around us.

Beyond simple description, language frames reality through inclusion, exclusion, and sequencing. We can create our own heroes and villains simply by choosing which portion of a story to convey or where we place our descriptive focus. Note, for instance, Kahneman's observations regarding hindsight and outcome bias:

> "Although hindsight and the outcome bias generally foster risk aversion, they also bring undeserved rewards to irresponsible risk seekers, such as a general or an entrepreneur who took a crazy gamble and won. Leaders who have been lucky are never punished for having taken too much risk. Instead, they are believed to have had the flair and foresight to anticipate success, and the sensible people who doubted them are seen in hindsight

as mediocre, timid, and weak. A few lucky gambles can crown a reckless leader with a halo of prescience and boldness."[257]

While Kahneman does not address language *per se*, his treatment of story is worth discussing here. When the stories we tell "are simple; are concrete rather than abstract; assign a larger role to talent, stupidity, and intentions than to luck; and focus on a few striking events that happened rather than on the countless events that failed to happen," we may end up maligning or venerating a particular individual without sufficient nuance.[258] Our capacity to tell complex stories is hindered by a number of different cognitive biases that tend to silence elements challenging our broader narrative. Inconsistencies are the enemy of simplicity and coherence.

We want a demon or a beacon of hope. We want a foolish, incompetent leader or an innovative genius. While we may consciously acknowledge multiple characteristics, we are not generally given to weaving a more complex story. As Kahneman notes, "…the statement 'Hitler loved dogs and little children' is shocking no matter how many times you hear it, because any trace of kindness in someone so evil violates the expectations set up by the halo effect."[259] Kahneman ultimately finds that, in the case of major events such as the 2008 financial crisis, the use of the word "know" is "perverse" because "the language implies that the world is more knowable than it is. It helps perpetuate a pernicious illusion."[260]

Language is often "interested" and conditioned by one's own perspective on the world. The way we describe the world around us is, in part, influenced by who we are and what we are trying to accomplish. Even those aspects of the world we decide to describe reveal something about the way in which we see the world.

To the extent that our descriptions of particular happenings in the world have broader influence, we must recognize that they, however accurate, may misrepresent reality. As we select what to communicate, we exert an influence on other people's perceptions of reality. As O'Connor and Wetherall note regarding journalism, "When Journalists share what they take to be most interesting—or of greatest interest to their readers—they can bias what the public sees in ways that ultimately mislead, even if they report only on real events."[261] Again, we see the power of language not simply in the manner in which we describe the world around us, but also in our choice of the aspects of the world we describe.

The power of language extends well beyond naming. Particularly in an age in which digital technologies allow the spread of ideas (false or true) through language, there is a great deal of potential for individuals or groups to speak without a great deal of accountability. Social media and other online publishing has created a situation in which propagating one's thoughts is as easy as having a casual conversation with a friend (in real life). Because we now have the opportunity to be more influential, those of us who choose to put our thoughts out into the world must do so recognizing the weight of the responsibility we take on in the context of "new power."

Reflections on Christians and Power (Particularly the Power of Language)

In all of this, what we find is a rather challenging context in which Christians must learn to use language theologically in order to tell theological stories. We have to think deeply about the way we use language and participate in discourse so that we convey what is actually there…the theological reality…with our language. If, as has been discussed above, language has the ability to shape one's perceptions of reality, use of language may be viewed as a Christian vocation in which we speak, write, and listen in ways that demonstrate a Christian social imaginary. The challenge of Christian speech is not limited to crafting formal doctrinal statements or creeds, but to theologically faithful articulations of all sorts.

Even if we choose to keep our thoughts to ourselves, we must exercise discernment as we decide whose ideas will influence our social vision of reality. In a world of digital media, we do not simply have the responsibility to speak Christianly, but to listen Christianly…to engage with the thoughts and opinions of others with a Christian mind deeply informed by the scriptures and sharpened by participation in and a commitment to an ecclesial community.

While we participate in this struggle, Bourdieu's language of imposition might suggest a coercive strategy incommensurate with Christian discourse. Imposing a social vision of reality on the world through coercive means is certainly not the goal of Christian use of language, yet as followers of Christ, we seek to convey a compelling social vision of the world aligned with the reality of the God described in the scriptures who is present and active among us. Our theological reality does not simply condition our message, *but the manner in which we convey it*. As such, if Christian participation with power through the use of language is to be intelligible as Christian, it must faithfully render a social vision of reality which acknowledges God without overdetermining who he is or what he is doing…without claiming that our language and actions somehow render God fully.

In *Graven Ideologies*, Benson highlights "three senses of separation and connection—knowing, doing and being related" noting "idols separate us from God, for they effectively act as a screen between God and us."[262] He goes on to focus on idols of a "conceptual nature" which are "either the creation or the adoption of a concept or idea that we take to be equivalent to God and thus worship as God."[263] Far from desiring Christians to be hindered from acting out their faith for fear of creating idols, Benson calls believers to exercise vigilance in avoiding the "misappropriation and distortion" of "good things" without becoming "so worried by the prospect of doing violence to God and to neighbor that one is left in inaction."[264]

The broader dynamic Benson seeks to reveal seems similar to Hauerwas's point regarding "the commonplace assumption that when people say 'God' they know what they are saying."[265] Hauerwas is not suggesting that God cannot be known, nor is he seeking to eliminate the possibility of describing God. Instead, as Benson notes concerning Nietzsche's perspective on simplicity and coherence, "whereas real life is characterized by complexity and variability, philosophers [and often theologians!] have attempted to tame reality by reducing it to simple, unchanging essences."²⁶⁶ In other words, simplistic paradigms capable of offering coherent explanations about a confused reality, however attractive they may be, have the potential to lure us into a false sense of security. It is this false sense of security that gives deconstruction its value. In "taking something apart very carefully in order to investigate its components" we engage in a process capable "of exposing something as a sham and, in so doing, destroying it" with the "natural effect of showing something to be questionable" so that "people will be less likely to believe it."²⁶⁷

Conclusion

As Christians use language and participate in the world, we would do well to engage in deconstructive thought in order to avoid the sort of conceptual idolatry Benson describes. While the logic of the digital age and the values of "new power" might suggest, for instance, that reporting on the failings of Christian leaders or institutions online is an act done by warriors for righteousness, Christians cannot ignore the possibility that we have adopted less-than virtuous mass media practices in the name of holding other Christians accountable…under the guise of seeking truth or crusading for justice.

It is not to say that engaging issues, seeking truth, holding one another accountable, or pursuing justice are not Christian activities. Such activities are appropriate at certain points within the life of Christ's body in the world. Yet, we must ensure that these activities do not create a conceptual idol defining God as none other than the one who authorizes these activities without restriction or limit. The Christian use of power, particularly the power of language, must always submit to the fact that true power…God's power…is conveyed through our weakness.

As Christians engage in discourse…as either speakers or listeners, writers or readers…we accept the responsibility to speak and listen with a Christian mind. We accept the responsibility to subject our speech to the sort of mind that (1) sees the unity of the body as something to which we must aspire, (2) refuses to dismiss God as absent or to somehow assume that the challenge of the moment is not his to solve, (3) resists the urge to accept without critical reflection the complex and varied perspectives and positions offered about a particular issue, and (4) feels no joy in the failings of God's people, but mourns and laments the fact that things are not as they are supposed to be. Christian discourse is not simply a matter of those who profess Christ having conversations with one another. It is the elevation of those conversations through a deep, multifaceted recognition that God exists and that our role in all areas of life is to bring glory to Him.

In considering Christian participation in power through language, it is perhaps most fitting to recall that such participation finds its goal in the ongoing articulation of theological reality. It is our responsibility and privilege to testify to God's presence with us and sovereign position over us. Such testimony is certainly challenged by the public sins of personas within the church, yet the challenge to that testimony will never be overcome by reactions that promote disunity. When we lose sight of the fact that the goal of any sort of accountability is restoration to fellowship, we create an undercurrent of condemnation less-than capable of conveying Christ to the world.

If we become a community that tells half truths, cannibalizes one another, or forgets that the shortcomings and willfully sinful acts of God's people are, at the same time, deeply lamentable and opportunities to showcase God's grace to a watching world, we will not demonstrate to the world what it means to have a truly Christian mind about one another. We will not show the world what it means to be a community which reflects deeply on the situations in which it finds itself. We will not admit our individual and communal need for repentance and change when we simply point a finger and put the weight of the world on a single individual or institution.

Using power through language with a Christian mind does not preclude confrontation of sin (far from it). We must hold one another accountable, be proactive in considering the implications of our actions, and slow down to reflect and pray. To do so requires that we acknowledge our own (often unwitting) participation in creating situations in which women, men, institutions, or even certain "watershed" issues have become fetishes…odd obsessions that distract us from the good work God is doing. While it is certainly the case that those in the limelight, those with elevated status and exposure in the community, are responsible for their own actions, those who speak and write about them are often as influential and certainly as culpable for the damage done when wielding words with power.

8 Terrible Simplification

Introduction

In 2003, I was carrying a load of mulch to my backyard to finish up some landscaping when I stepped in a hole. The combination of the load I was carrying and the sudden twist that occurred when I stepped in the hole was quite painful. Being a twenty-six year old in relatively good shape, I shook it off and kept working. The next day, I woke up with sharp pains in my hip. After a few rounds of ibuprofen had no effect, I headed to the doctor who offered an initial diagnosis of bursitis (a swelling of the bursa in my hip joint) and prescribed steroids. He also made sure to tell me that if the pain did not decrease in a day or two, I needed to come back. It didn't. After a few more attempts to fix what presented as a hip issue, I went in for an MRI and discovered a herniated disc and two bulging discs in my lumbar spine.

I dealt with my back issues for another nine years. Pain killers weren't an option since I still wanted to function, so I was in and out of physical therapy and tried my best to avoid situations where I might exacerbate the injury. By 2012, the pain had become unbearable. It would take me several minutes to stand up from a seated position and it felt like someone was jamming a knife into the bottom of my foot most of the time. I ended up having a partial discectomy to remove the bad portions of the herniated disc, alleviate the pain, and, ultimately, help to preserve the rest of the discs in my back which would have been adversely impacted by removing the disc completely and fusing the vertebrae. After nine years, the underlying physical cause of the pain had to be addressed…the symptoms could no longer be managed.

Solving "problems" in the church is similar to the situation I went through with my back. We often feel some sort of pain in a particular locale. We know where it hurts. Based on that information, we make an initial diagnosis, which, at times, ends up being wrong. Once we actually identify the problem, we limp along trying to manage the pain and avoid more drastic measures for as long as possible. We manage the problem rather than fixing it because we believe (perhaps rightly) that fixing the problem will lead to greater damage down the road. We know, however, that managing the problem and minimizing its effects isn't a strategy we can sustain forever. At some point, the pain becomes too great and we have to resolve the underlying issue, which has often, by that point, become less of a problem and more of a crisis.

Worse yet, it is often the case that even when we identify a problem rightly, we become so fixated on alleviating pain in the moment that we neglect the set of factors that predisposed us to developing the problem in the first place. Take the story of my back as an example. While the most immediate cause was a hole, it wasn't the root cause. Saying that I don't enjoy yard work probably isn't strong enough…I loathe it. My goal when I am forced to landscape, mow, or plant anything is to get it done as quickly as possible.

On the day I hurt my back, we were waiting on a wheelbarrow that my dad had gone to the store to purchase. I got impatient and angry (not an isolated incident…I had a rather short fuse back then), filled up a large garbage can with mulch, and began carrying it to the back yard. That oversized garbage can filled with mulch is what I was carrying when I stepped in the hole and, ultimately, injured my back. While I ended up with a back problem, which I was rather diligent about caring for, I ignored my anger issues (even blaming my ongoing anger issues on the pain) for another ten years.

When we focus on the current crisis or what is causing us pain at a given moment, we run the risk of missing the proverbial forrest for the trees. We end up ignoring the conditions that put us at a greater risk of developing the pain we now feel in the first place. We wait for the crisis, address it, weather whatever challenges it brings, and move on without ever really making the necessary changes to avoid the problem, or others like it, in the future. This situation denies deeper, slower conversations. Such conversations, while requiring diligence, patience, and a willingness to endure pain, might allow us to avoid the sort of oversimplifications that only preserve the church's underlying status quo.

The maintenance of the status quo may be encouraged by any number of factors. Two of those factors seem to me to be rather prevalent: (1) terribly simple accounts offering inadequate descriptions of a specific situation and (2) an underdeveloped ecclesiology resulting in the illusion that retaining the status quo is crucial to the church's survival. These factors are not exclusively responsible for human tendencies to overemphasize certain problems while overlooking others. The impulse we have to bring closure and coherence to a situation and to reestablish the "normal" way of things is motivated by a host of other conscious and unconscious factors. Resisting the temptation to proclaim that we have adequately engaged an issue or that in seeking truth we have somehow now found it, is an appropriate, necessary Christian struggle.

To offer a short midrash on Romans 8, we do not always know what we are looking for, but rely on the Spirit's intercession to fill in our own gaps in knowledge and understanding as He translates our unintelligible groanings. We are inherently limited in our understanding of just how God will work things together for our good…how the various sufferings we endure will produce in us the character that leads to glorification. When we tell simple stories and pretend that we understand what should be done or how God is moving, we tell, more often than not, a misleading tale of God's interactions with the world. We neglect the Spirit's ministry proceeding to address the pains we know. In essence, becoming impatient as we wait for God's intervention, we opt to solve the problems we can see and, perhaps too often, being satisfied with our solutions. We make things terribly simple.

plicity

When Burckhardt coined the term "terrible simplifiers" he was describing those in Ancient Greece who would advance an agenda by leveraging legitimate mechanisms for decision-making to serve their own agendas. He recognized that many of the orators took advantage of the position they had in society to move the masses in ways that were of benefit to the orators. Note, for instance, his comments regarding Athens and its orators:

> "The most repellant feature of Athens in the time of the orators is the way the popular assembly and the courts, with all their official apparatus, were the setting for the worst chicanery and persecutions, and provided the means for them. When we contemplate all the corrupt orators, the mass of decisions never put into practice, the claques and noisemakers to drown protests, the sycophants and false witnesses, the entanglement of the innocent in criminal proceedings, the silencing by murder of those who had right on their side, what amazes us is the immense arrogance of this unashamed parading of evil."[268]

Burckhardt is not overly gracious in his assignment of pernicious motives to the orators. It would seem appropriate to recognize a spectrum of motives ranging from intentional deception to well-meaning, though misled, influence. In other words, terrible simplification does not only arise from mustache-twisting power mongers with an appetite for world domination. It also arises from those who, in seeking to make a positive contribution of some sort, so limit their perspective that the solutions for which they advocate only serve to reinforce or exacerbate the problem they are trying to solve.[269]

Terribly simple accounts utilize limited information to craft a coherent story that conveys a convincing view of the world.[270] They systematize and simplify by ignoring or denying aspects of a particular situation that do not fit the simple story they are advancing. They domesticate a "wicked problem" which may be understood as "a complex issue that defies complete definition, for which there can be no final solution, since any resolution generates further issues, and where solutions are not true or false or good or bad, but the best that can be done at the time." Terrible simplification serves to advance solutions that may or may not be "the best that can be done at the time."[271]

This sort of terrible simplification often alleviates or numbs enough of the pain to allow the status quo to be effectively *sustained*. Such an effect is especially likely because of the terrible simplification of theology in both its more popular forms if not in academic discourse. The claim that theology has become terribly simple says less about theology than it does about those who make theology too (terribly) simple. In some instances, theology becomes analogous to ideology when it "makes it unnecessary for people to confront individual issues on their individual merits."[272]

Theology can become a sort of "prepared formulae" applied broadly to a specific situation with little to no regard for the contours and complexities…the unique historical circumstances…of that situation. Similarly, there is little to no regard for the multifaceted ways in which various streams of theological thought might have relevance. Perhaps worse than this use of theology is the relative scarcity of voices that call it into question, particularly in its more popular manifestations.

A Terribly Simple Moment

While I am less prepared to label individuals or groups as "terrible simplifiers," it seems appropriate to highlight instances of terrible simplicity. A ready example of which I am familiar may be found in John MacArthur's conversation with Ben Shapiro.[273] In speaking about the challenges related to choosing between candidates for political office, Shapiro asks "As religious people, how should we choose between candidates who may not be personally moral but may forward our priorities, or do we disengage completely?" MacArthur's response would likely qualify as being "terribly simple" particularly in two lines of thought.

First, he hones in on a single, biblical issue (i.e. abortion) noting that the choice of candidates is "challenging…but it is less challenging than it used to be" because "you have a party that advocates the killing of babies. I can't vote that. I don't care who the other guy is." At the same time, MacArthur acknowledges that in society we are always choosing between "the lesser of two evils…because nobody is perfect."

Second, he describes the office of the presidency a requiring "a certain skillset for leadership" which includes "a certain ability people need to effect change." He underscores the significance of competence through an analogy with brain surgery: "If a brain surgeon is going to open my brain, I'm not too concerned about his moral life. I would like to know that he's been in somebody else's brain and he's done the right thing when he's been there." He goes on to suggest that the presidency is "not a moral job" or a "position of moral authority. It never was and we don't want to make it into that now."[274] He notes that the president should be the "best you've got" which he describes as someone who "does justice, fears God…that is to say there is a transcendental ought that binds his heart. An atheist doesn't have that. Even the founders of America who were not Christians…they were deists…knew God had to be in there somewhere."

MacArthur does qualify his explanations noting the decline of several other social structures that are contributing to the tearing of America's social fabric. In this manner, MacArthur's answers point to a more complex solution. He does not see that everything falls at the feet of the president, but recognizes a more limited scope of presidential practice. In speaking of the restoration of moral authority in the culture he assigns responsibility to individuals and groups. MacArthur leans back on the moral authority of Scripture and advocates for an approach that seeks to proclaim the Bible's authority to shape public opinion.

MacArthur's comments, however, illustrate the sort of dynamics involved in terrible simplification. For instance, MacArthur disqualifies the entire Democratic Party (presumably) on moral grounds due to the party's pro-choice advocacy and then goes on to suggest that the presidency is not and has never been a "moral job" or "position of moral authority." He diminishes moral criteria in his analogy of the brain surgeon noting that he is 'not too concerned" with the brain surgeon's "moral life," yet he eliminates the Democratic Party as a pro-choice party (also an oversimplification) out of hand on moral grounds.[275]

True, he qualifies this issue noting that the "best you've got" should be someone concerned with justice and who has a "transcendental ought that binds his heart." Presumably, MacArthur would argue that this "transcendental ought" is lacking in politicians who hold the pro-choice position. If such is the case, it is not readily apparent why it is that this "transcendental ought" criteria would be used in relation to pro-choice candidates and not in relation to candidates who, for instance, speak in a vulgar manner about women, have extramarital affairs, exhibit a love of money, or actively seek to reinforce structural evils of various sorts. The challenge, then, is not that MacArthur is wrong to assert that the Bible offers definitive, authoritative perspectives with regard to matters of abortion, the sanctity of marriage, or the significance of the family. Instead, the challenge is that he does not justify why such matters crowd out other concerns about which the scriptures also speak with authority.

Beyond specific political choices on which many well-meaning Christians would likely differ there are also concerns with some of his underlying claims. For instance, even if we assume that the presidency is not a "position of moral authority," we cannot deny the impact the president has as a symbol of the nation, its citizens, and the various sorts of values the voting populace affirm. MacArthur's brain surgeon analogy serves to underscore the point that an amateur brain surgeon with high moral character would certainly be less-than desirable. However, to suggest that skills can be disentangled and treated as wholly separate from morality does not respect the complex individual and social interactions bound up with leadership more generally.

In this specific response within the context of the interview, MacArthur uses a terribly simple story to address what is an extremely complex issue. His conviction regarding pro-choice stances is clear enough; however, in bracketing out an entire segment of the political community (which would not be limited to a specific political party, nor all encompassing of the political party he appears to reference) on moral grounds, MacArthur plays into broad generalizations. These generalizations reinforce polarized perspectives that are arguably part of the bigger problem with American politics and Christian discourse generally.

MacArthur's argument seems clear on the surface, but, upon closer examination, does not do justice to the ambiguity and complexity involved in the issues he addresses. For instance, why focus on the issues of abortion, transgender policy, or gay marriage to the exclusion of other acts of sexual immorality, fiscal policy and practice, lewd speech, or campaign fundraising? His assertion that the scriptures speak authoritatively on the former matters is correct. The terrible simplification comes as we (over)emphasize abortion, gay marriage, and gender identity matters as *the* watershed biblical issues about which Christians should be concerned.

Can we really say that inappropriate handling of wealth, sexual impropriety between a man and a woman outside of marriage, or acts that diminish or disenfranchise those made in God's image are not matters about which Christians might be concerned and which might impact decisions regarding candidates for political office? Could not these or other issues trump positions on abortion or transgender policy? Perhaps MacArthur would not deny that such matters should also be taken into account, yet, the manner in which he answers Shapiro's question about one's choice of political candidates certainly appears to elevate one issue (abortion) or set of issues (abortion, gay rights, and gender identity legislation) above all others.

I use this example not in an attempt to defame John MacArthur. I'm not familiar with the full corpus of MacArthur's work, so my only real frame of reference for his views is the interview with Shapiro. In the portion of the interview noted above, MacArthur's "terrible simplification" lies in his elevation of a narrow set of issues as determinative criteria for evaluating the legitimacy of a political party or candidate. His emphasis on this narrow set of positions, as well as his focus on more traditional family values and the reestablishment of a particular social fabric suggest the need for Christian affiliation with the Republican Party. There is a simple solution to a complex problem: choosing political candidates is "less challenging" than in the past because Christians can bracket out one of the parties in what is functionally a two party system.[276]

Why is such terrible simplification problematic? **First**, this sort of simplification offers an incomplete, though not necessarily false, treatment of the issue at hand. Is the matter of a candidate's position on abortion important? Surely it is, but it is not the only matter of importance. It is not the sole criteria that Christians might take into account in determining what political candidate to choose. Terrible simplifications narrow our field of vision in ways that tend to diminish (a) our awareness of other factors and/or (b) our capacity to evaluate them as significant to articulating a public Christian testimony.

Second, terrible simplification describes a problem or situation in a manner that excludes other frames. In approaching his response through the framework of abortion, traditional family values and structures, and the establishment of a beneficial social order, MacArthur is treading on familiar theological ground. His perspective need not be rejected, but, like other perspectives, it must be recognized as incomplete. He offers important insights…but not final, authoritative insights. MacArthur's comments regarding the choice of political candidates appears to be driven by at least three factors: (a) a particular understanding of government, (b) participation in contemporary American politics, and (c) a particular desire for and view of social order. These factors are far from pernicious on their own, but they do not include other, potentially significant factors that might, were they to be made more prominent in the discussion, change the manner in which Christians interact with politics in America.

For instance, what about the issue of unity in the body of Christ? While the "good of the (secular) order" may well be important, the promotion of unity within the church is certainly a Christian concern. So, perhaps the unity of the body of Christ could frame the manner in which Christians participate in politics. How might we change the way we think about elections, about conversations regarding various political positions, or about affiliation with a particular party were we to approach these questions with the goal of promoting the unity of the church? Recent tensions regarding social justice and the gospel, in which MacArthur was also involved, have certainly not held the unity of the church up as a particularly high value. Instead, terrible simplifications of biblical authority and the gospel have been put forth apart from concerns related to the unity of the church or the practice of mutual respect within the body of Christ.

Third, terrible simplifications yield distorted theological narratives. Narrowing the solution, particularly when that solution incorporates Scripture or relies on a particular theological concept, diminishes the varied, multifaceted ways in which God works within the community of faith and the world more broadly. Terrible simplifications tend to present God as a character whose actions are fully intelligible (or close to fully intelligible) to those who understand the scriptures. Often these terrible simplifications tell the story of a god who is all too often allied with those who wish to preserve or bring about a particular state of things. This sort of story…this theological narrative…presents a god limited in options and, at times, subject to human agendas.

Finally, terrible simplification creates the illusion that a decision-making process is adequate and that there is no need to reflect on it. Bahcall addresses this dynamic in his comparison of an outcome versus a system mindset suggesting, "System mindset means carefully examining the quality of decisions, not just the quality of outcomes."[277] He goes on to describe the challenge of the more simplistic and ambiguous focus on outcomes noting, "A failed outcome…does not necessarily mean the decision or decision process behind it was bad. There are good decisions with bad outcomes…Evaluating decisions and outcomes separately is equally important in the opposite case: bad decisions may occasionally result in good outcomes."[278] Terrible simplification can often be served by an emphasis on outcomes rather than on approaches that evaluate both the outcomes and the processes of which outcomes are the effect.

Underdeveloped Ecclesiology

Structural Evil

One person's comfortable status quo is another person's place of tension and struggle. We live in a world that is not right...even those of us who are currently comfortable are not experiencing the world as it ought to be. Our reinforcement of the status quo and the accompanying "structures of sin" do not arise solely from the evil intentions and actions of humankind, but "come also through ignorant if well-intentioned choices...They become forces in the universe beyond the control of the individuals involved, often compelling their collusion."[279] Gutiérrez is perhaps even more pointed in his comments regarding the characterization of the situation in Latin America as a "situation of sin" noting that such a description "not only criticizes the individual abuses on the part of those who enjoy great power in this social order; it calls into question their uses of power, that is to say, it is a repudiation of the whole existing system—to which the church itself belongs."[280]

Even if the term is not used, "structural evil" has become increasingly prominent in discussions of immigration, race relations in the church, economics, and environmental concerns. Though it is certainly appropriate to speak of structural evil in relation to these topics, it would be a mistake to limit the concept to these areas alone. Structural evil may be best understood as a given social configuration or social imaginary constituted by assumptions, habits, cultural practices, policies, or institutions that threaten to conform us (whether individually or collectively) to the image of something *other than Christ*. Structural sin exists in the gaps of social imaginaries that do not or cannot take into account (1) all of the ways in which we have become connected to others worldwide and (2) the manner in which we might change, for instance, our grocery shopping habits, in order to somehow do less harm in the world while still being able to participate in social life, particularly in the Western world and the United States.

Outside of the economic and ecological arena, one may find rather clear instances of structural evil in the global epidemic of sex trafficking. In a powerful treatment of the matter, Kara highlights the "global magnitude of victimization of young women" reminding readers that "every minute of every day, the most vulnerable women and children in the world are raped for profit with impunity..."[281] While tempting to think that it is only those who participate (willingly or unwillingly) in the sex trade who are degraded, our casual acceptance of the world as it is, our attempts to change without losing too much, and our seeming unwillingness to add variables and complexity to our conversations impact all of us...making us all complicit to the extent that we choose to believe that *the world is less wrong than it actually is*. We all play a role, wittingly or unwittingly, in reinforcing the fallen nature of God's creation.

It is not so much that our "petty" issues pale in comparison to other global problems like the sex trade. Instead, we have to be willing to reevaluate our system in its entirety rather than making small adjustments to preserve what is and to set aside the harder problems that "what is" can't solve. Rather than elevating a particular issue to the top of the pile and demoting others to the bottom, it may be necessary to recognize the possibility that the issues we face are in some way conditioned by the social arrangements...the underlying social imaginaries...that reinforce the manner in which we exist in the world and, perhaps worse, prepare others to exist in the world.

Hauerwas' response to whether, after Vatican II, "we should be more ecumenical and see the good in all faiths" demonstrates the sort of systemic issues that reinforce the status quo even beyond a single generation. He notes, "The great enemy of the church today is not atheism but sentimentality; and there's no deeper sentimentality than the presumption by Christians and nonbelievers alike that they should be able to have children without their children suffering for their convictions."[282] In pointing to "sentimentality,"

Hauerwas points not to a particular problem, but to an underlying understanding or disposition toward reality.

Even as we evaluate our systems, it is important to remember that, for Christians, "doing what we can" does not always mean we are doing what we should. There are a myriad of unsolvable problems around us. The body of Christ and its members are to exhibit compassion, hospitality, and generosity…we are to love God and neighbor. At the same time, we must exercise a great deal of discernment as we consider Christian participation in broader systemic change. Perhaps developing more robust practices of corporate prayer and lament would sharpen our understanding of the problems facing the church and make it less intelligible for us to engage in, activities that not only divide us, but keep God at arm's length.

Structural Evil and Ecclesiology

Structural evil and the maintenance of the status quo are underwritten by an underdeveloped ecclesiology, or, perhaps a fundamental misunderstanding of what it means to be the church. The church is not an institution…it is a collective of individuals united in Christ.[283] This collective has been freed for service to Christ and to one another through the crucifixion and resurrection of Jesus. The church operates in accordance with the scriptures empowered and prompted by the Spirit to witness, worship, and serve in diverse and distinct settings around the world. It is a coordinated, connected community with a peculiar character and mission accomplished by individual and collective acting and speaking within the world for the glory of God.[284]

Understanding the church as something other than an institution with building funds and monthly budgets is crucial to overcoming human tendencies toward the status quo. In *Antifragile*, Taleb highlights the challenge of path dependent thinking and the manner in which many business men focus too quickly on success and too little on survival. He suggests, "This fragility that comes from path dependence is often ignored by business men who, trained in static thinking, tend to believe that generating profits is their principle mission, with survival and risk control something to perhaps consider—they miss the strong logical precedence of survival over success. To make profits and buy a BMW, it would be a good idea to, first, survive."[285]

Taleb's point is an important one for those running finite organizations that can actually end. Businesses, institutions of higher education, non-profit ministries, and individual churches all have finite life-spans…they will all end. The body of Christ, as a multi-generational, multi-cultural collective of individuals organically connected to one another through Christ *is not finite*. The body of Christ is sustained by God's faithfulness and will endure against any and all odds. The "path dependent thinking" that Taleb describes…the need to account for survival and risk control before focusing on profits and outcomes…has already been addressed for the body of Christ. A rightly structured ecclesiology recognizes that while members of the body are vulnerable to this-worldly threats, the existence of the body of Christ is never in any ultimate danger.

Without a concern for ultimate survival, the body of Christ as a whole and the individual members of it are free to take risks for the gospel. The challenge for the body of Christ is to avoid preoccupations with finite structures that will end. Allowing inertia to propel an organization or institution forward even when God's blessing is no longer upon it does not serve the body of Christ. In fact, the rather challenging dynamics that exist between institution and individual were, in part, expressed in the new covenant.

As Israel's communal and governmental mechanisms failed due to long-term faithlessness without repentance, Israel's people were enlisted to preserve the traditions that were no longer being carried out by the nation on an organizational level. These individuals were not called to divorce themselves from God's law, but to recognize the distinction between God's law, the wisdom it conveys, and the institutions that had been constructed to govern (unsuccessfully) Israelite life and practice. How we might go about discerning that it is time for an organization or institution to be set aside is a separate question, which may be answered, in part, by reconsidering the way we make our decisions as a local body in relation to the body of Christ more broadly.

For instance, the so-called "higher education crisis" occurring due to a variety of changes in student demographics, cultural perceptions of higher education's value, and increasing costs has the makings of becoming the next "to big to fail" industry. While there are certainly good reasons to retain Christian colleges, Bible Colleges, and seminaries, we must also recognize that the higher education structure is a relatively recent phenomenon within the history of the church. The fact that the church was not started with (and was able to survive for the bulk of its history without) higher education suggests that Christian higher education is a situated solution (a technology) that provided a needed mechanism for Christian education given certain social, cultural and economic factors.

Higher education has its strengths, but it is not essential to the body of Christ. Education, which I would tend to understand as a subset of discipleship, may well be bound up with the mission of the church and the formation of individual Christians.[286] The academic disciplines, the institutionalized structures of higher education and accreditation, and the professionalized guild of scholars, strengthen the body of Christ in many ways. At the same time, when understood as non-negotiable structures without which the church cannot accomplish its core mission of making disciples, these finite structures can limit the church's imagination and preoccupy its time and resources. We become distracted and set aside our core mission of making disciples to sustain structures that may have served their purpose.[287]

Part of the solution to this problem, is to develop a more robust ecclesiology. Such an ecclesiology must recognize that a deep commitment to theological practice is not necessarily a solution to the world's (or church's) problems, but is a necessary condition for the church to be the church and to get on with the mission of making disciples. Living with deep commitment is a "good process" that may not yield "good outcomes" (at least in the near term). The practice of making disciples involves forming ourselves into a community of women and men for whom the presence and reign of God are theological realities rather than mere theological maxims or pithy Christian slang for "everything will be ok" or "God is in control."

Such an ecclesiology is not isolating, but exhibits movement and engagement. It is not the case that theological practice only involves prayer in dark rooms or intense Bible study in musty libraries. Rather, theological practice involves the proclamation of the gospel through a comprehensive Christian testimony lived out in the lives of the body's members. It is an all-encompassing ecclesiology that includes not just what it means to be human, but what it means to embody Christ after his resurrection.

Focusing in on ecclesiology and theological practice offers a different sort of grid through which to evaluate the status quo. It is not only a matter of implementing a set of biblical principles or following a set of rules for life. Rather, Christian testimony informed by a robust ecclesiology understands that theological practice is a unifying activity designed to strengthen the body of Christ by pointing to the character of God and the manner in which his faithfulness and power has created an "antifragile" church. When we rightly understand the church as a people empowered by the Spirit to demonstrate what it means to live with God, the theological practices of lament, repentance, confession, sacrifice, generosity, forgiveness, patience, prayer, humility, confrontation and a host of others begin to come to us more naturally. As such disciplines reorient our instincts to a new vision of reality, we will only be more capable of moving faithfully within a broken world.

Conclusion

When we content ourselves with addressing the presenting concerns of the day, we deny ourselves the opportunities that come with confronting the depths of our own incompleteness, insanity, and deception. Reinforcing our own delusions provides only the façade of comfort and only the appearance of faithfulness. Reading the scriptures, meditating on the word of God, and learning to delight in God's law requires us to open ourselves up to deep, transformative change. Proclaiming the power of God's word demands that we subject the whole of who we are, both individually and collectively, to the work of God.

9 Accountability In Fresh Perspective

Introduction

"Do you have an accountability partner?" Coming up through Campus Crusade in the late 1990's, the "accountability partner" question was pretty common. The assumption (a right one I think) is that we need others in our lives to keep us on the "straight and narrow." Yet, accountability extends well beyond behavior modification (or at least it should). To be held accountable is to be challenged to conform the whole of who we are to the image of Christ…to live a cruciform life within the context of Christ's body.

Accountability is surely an act of friendship done amongst the members of the community of faith in so much as those to whom we are united in Christ show themselves unwilling to let us suffer the consequences of our own agendas, rebellions, and inadequacies without some sort of intervention. Viewing accountability as an act of friendship alone, however, is theologically limiting. Such a focus on the interpersonal aspects of accountability cannot be allowed to diminish accountability's corporate dimensions. It seems clear that accountability has corporate implications, yet it is less clear that sufficient measures have been taken to ensure corporate accountability.

Our union with Christ forges organic connections between us and each of the other members of Christ's body. We are individually connected both to Christ and to the rest of the members of the community of faith.

Accountability cannot be limited to isolated moral behavior because we do not exist as isolated moral individuals. Accountability is not solely a matter of ensuring an abstract personal piety, but of cultivating theologically fitting behavior situated within the matrix of relationships established as a consequence of union with Christ.

The scriptures reveal God as one whose character and covenantal relationship with his people demand and empower holiness. There are behaviors incommensurate with the Christian life, in part, because they deny God's wisdom and misrepresent God to the world. While God prohibits certain behaviors outright, in other matters God's people are left to discern what it means to embody God's wisdom. There is no recipe to follow as we confront the challenges of daily life.

That process of discernment is guided by a theo-logic developed through intimate, ongoing interactions with the word and Spirit which "cultivate not only new thoughts but *habits* of thought, a way of thinking in accordance with the gospel."[288] In Romans 14, Paul highlights a particular theo-logic that begins with love for sisters and brothers in Christ and is continually guided by a concern not to "destroy the one for whom Christ died" (Rom 14:15). Paul's theo-logic is rooted in the conviction that "the kingdom of God is not a matter of eating and drinking but of righteousness and peace and joy in the Holy Spirit" (14:17).

Despite the fact that "nothing is unclean in itself," it does not follow that Christians can eat anything they choose *because Christians must attend to their relationships within the community of faith*. Something that may be otherwise appropriate can become taboo if it creates "a stumbling block or hindrance in the way of a brother" (14:13). This way of discerning a theologically fitting action suggests that there are layers to accountability that need to be further explored. Accountability is not solely concerned with ensuring that explicit prohibitions are not violated, but with the evaluation of how one's behavior impacts others within the body of Christ.

In 1 Corinthians 12, Paul addresses the character of the body noting, "God arranged the members in the body, each one of them, as he chose" (18). Paul emphasizes the necessary diversity of the unified body by highlighting the peculiar distribution of honor as the means of precluding the body's division: "…God has so composed the body, giving greater honor to the part that lacked it, that there may be no division in the body, but that the members may have the same care for one another" (24-25). Reflecting on this section from the standpoint of accountability, it is possible to understand more clearly the need to address broader structural concerns within the community of faith.

A hand cannot think of itself more highly than it ought, nor can it diminish the ear, eye, foot, or any other part of the body. The hand is a hand…it is not the first among equals or worthy of any honor beyond that which God has designated. Commenting on 1 Corinthians 12, Schreiner notes that the interdependence of the various members of the body leaves, "…no room for self-promotion, for an exclusive spirit denies the unity and diversity of the body."[289] Any given member of the body has worth. They each exercise different functions within the body as a whole for the good of the body as a whole.

The body's members have a designated place and function within the body of Christ that would not be effectively exercised apart from the rest of the body's members. There is an order inherent within God's arrangement of the body that no individual member or collective discernment of the group may disrupt. In the body of Christ, there is no sense that any member is the "first among equals," nor is there one part that is given unfettered dominance within the body because "…Christ is the head of the church, his body, and is himself its Savior" (Eph 5:23; cf. Col 1:18). Part of what needs to be considered in matters of accountability, then, involves the ongoing preservation of the order given to the body's members. Such preservation requires that attention be given to the arrangements between members of the body. It also requires the church to consider how actions that may be otherwise appropriate skew distributions of honor within the Christian community, thus becoming potential sites of division.

Accountability assumes not only adherence to a set of morals and personal piety, but also a willingness to accept one's God-given position as a member of Christ's body in relation to other members of that body, as well as using the spiritual gifts granted to us for the building up of the body. Accountability assumes a willingness to act so as to maximize the contribution of the body as a whole rather than maximizing one's own individual actions to the detriment of the body's other parts. Life in community is not a matter of abstract morals or ethics, but of nurturing the health of the whole body even if it means depriving ourselves of good things to do so. To hold one another accountable, then, requires that we consider the repercussions of individual and collective behaviors and activities on the various members within the body of Christ.

Toward a "Skin-in-the-Game Sort of Accountability

In *Skin in the Game: Hidden Asymmetries in Daily Life*, Nassim Taleb categorizes people into three broad categories. **First**, there are those with skin in the game. These are people who preach and practice…they take their own advice. They don't tell you to bet on red when they intend to bet on black (or, more likely, not to bet at all). An example of this sort of person might be an entrepreneur who puts his or her own money on the line to take a chance on an idea or a business. **Second**, there are those who *don't* have skin in the game. These are individuals who reap the benefits ("the upside") without a commensurate risk of failure ("the downside"). Consultants, for instance, have far less downside than the full-time employees of the company for which they consult because when the recommendations the consultant has made don't yield strong results he or she will already have moved on to another consulting engagement. **Finally**, there are those who have their soul in the game. These are people who take on more than their fair share of risk for others. These are the firemen who run into burning buildings, individuals who expose falsehood and scandal to their own detriment, and those who give their lives for others (e.g. Jesus).

While Taleb does not talk about the typology in terms of Christian accountability, there is something beneficial about understanding accountability in terms of having "skin in the game" which would entail taking on "upside" and "downside" or foregoing "upside" to take on additional "downside" for others. Understanding accountability in these terms seems particularly helpful when considering how accountability might occur for prominent Christians whose ministries are not limited to a single local congregation. Prominent Christian writers, speakers, pastors, journalists, singers, comedians, etc. need to ask themselves whether they really have skin in the game or whether they are reaping an "upside" while others take on all or most of the risk for "downside."

Having "skin in the game" is about putting oneself at risk of experiencing downside. As a member of the community of faith, however, having "skin in the game" entails more than just putting oneself at risk. "Skin in the game" within the church means recognizing that one's own "upside" may result in "downside" for other members of the community. It isn't simply about putting one's own self at risk of downside, but about leaving open the possibility of surrendering one's own upside when that upside is detrimental to other members of the body of Christ.

Consider an analogy related to our physical body. It is possible to develop a strong chest by doing lifts like the bench press in the weight room. The chest has a particular role and function in the movement of the shoulder joint. There are a number of benefits to having a strong chest, but overemphasizing chest development while neglecting supporting muscles such as those of the rotator cuff, upper- and mid-back, and the posterior shoulder creates a scenario in which the body is more prone to injury. A strong chest alone does not a healthy body make.

Our physical bodies are made up of diverse parts all of which contribute to the functioning of our bodies as a whole. The church is no different. One member may be able to make substantial gains while others do not. An individual member, however, does not function in isolation from the rest of the body, nor can that member perform at his or her peak when other members of the body are weak or suffering. Each member of the body of Christ must attend to the body as a whole recognizing that they do not function autonomously. In short, every member has a stake in seeing the body of Christ thrive…whether they recognize it or not.

Thinking about Accountability in Skin-in-the-Game Terms

That a dynamic already exists in which some Christians have upside with little to no downside or whose upside enhances the downside for others may be hypothetically considered via the case of a prominent pastor with broad influence in the church. Consider a prominent pastor with a syndicated radio program, multiple books, podcasts, frequent speaking engagements, and tens of thousands of followers on social media. There is nothing inherently wrong with prominence, nothing evil about having a radio program, authoring books, or speaking at conferences. Yet, while there may not be anything inherently wrong with attaining prominence (God often gives members of the body influential platforms), there has been too little thought about the impact prominence has on the rest of the community of faith.

Consider the following "what if…" scenario. As the influence of a given pastor grows, he or she requests that the community of faith support his or her radio ministry, buy his or her books, and subscribe to his or her podcast. Meanwhile, the local church pastor is working 80 hours a week to care for a congregation whose members weigh and measure him against the prominent pastor only to find their local pastor lacking in comparison to his more prominent counterpart. In this situation, the prominent pastor has a great deal of upside and relatively little downside.

The prominent pastor is capable of reaching the masses, having an influence, and funding a large ministry. The prominent pastor enjoys the privileges (and responsibilities) that come with being a voice for the community of faith proclaiming the word of God and calling "balls and strikes" on a wide range of topics that may or may not be settled by the scriptures. Yet, the prominent pastor seldom has to deal with the struggles and challenges that come up in the lives of his or her fans and followers. That is left to local pastors whose upsides are dwarfed by downsides related to money, resources, respect, and a host of other issues.

The prominent pastor's upside may well create *more* downside for local church pastors. Are resources that might otherwise come to the local church being diverted? Are already problematic congregants given knowledge without discipleship? Does the conversational agenda driven within broader Christian dialogue distract local congregations from issues of greater concern within their particular community? Perhaps…perhaps not. The point is not to condemn prominent pastors or to speak against influential Christians and their ministries. Rather, the point is that these are questions worth asking as we consider what it means to hold one another accountable to maintain the order of the body of Christ.

Consider another "what if…" scenario. A journalist publishes stories of scandals at Christian organizations with the intent of bringing about reform. The journalist, sitting outside of the organization, has low downside and the potential for tremendous upside by engaging a largely uninformed public with sensational news. Leaders within the organization with the supposed scandal are also largely without downside, particularly in Christian non-profit organizations in which board members are not financially dependent on the organization for their livelihoods. Those who realize the downside are not those who lead the organization, but those within the organization who perform specific roles to accomplish the organization's mission.

When the journalist exposes so-called corruption, leadership engages the public relations machine, pacifies the angry mob so that the pitchforks and torches are put away, and everyone moves on with life. The journalist gets to put one in the "win" column, gains new followers, and moves on to expose a new scandal. Organizational leadership gets to "solve a problem" in the public eye and continue with business as usual after weathering a couple of bumps in the road. Neither the leadership or the journalist has effected the sort of change that would improve the upside for those within the organization. Those within Christian organizations who would prefer not to leave or would suffer considerable loss by doing so experience the downside of public scandal most acutely. The workers within an organization experience more than their fair share of the downside while institutional leadership and journalists find greater "upside."

There are a number of other "what if…" scenarios that might be considered, but the point is that once someone gains prominence and is allowed to have more upside than downside, accountability becomes a challenge. In part, the dynamics created by having more upside than downside are the reason that those who are truly thinking Christianly demand to be held accountable themselves. If the body of Christ is truly interested in holding its members accountable, we need to be asking different questions that reflect a new understanding of accountability. If what we mean by accountability is that, having been caught cheating, a poker player with a large pile of chips can no longer place bets, but must cash out and go roll around in his or her substantial pile of ill-gotten money, we can achieve accountability without addressing the balance between risk (downside) and reward (upside).

If, as I have suggested, it is challenging to hold those without skin in the game accountable, we need to consider how we might avoid situations in which members of the body of Christ have no skin in the game. Let's not put members of the body of Christ in positions where they become functionally immune to accountability. Ensuring that no individual member or group within the body operates without sufficient "skin in the game" has to become a priority…a point of serious reflection as we consider how the body of Christ is structured in a digital age. There has to be an intentional effort made to maximize the body of Christ as a whole by evaluating the influence and activities of various members in light of the way those members impact others.

Understanding accountability in this manner results in rather different problems that require expanding sets of proposed solutions adapted to a given scenario and environment. Not every accountability problem is one that entails individual incompetence or sin of some sort. Whatever else such solutions may entail, they must address the theological fittingness of members who assume the privileges of leadership without accepting the accompanying responsibilities of a leader (perhaps the definition of having no skin in the game). Addressing accountability in terms of "upside" and "downside" offers the opportunity to cultivate different perspectives about how we might reconfigure and reorient the Christian community in ways that would allow the body of Christ to minister more faithfully together.

The examples offered concerning the prominent pastor and Christian "whistle blower" are not intended as condemnations, but as illustrations of the sort of dynamics related to accountability that often go unaddressed. Influential pastors and Christian media personalities are important members of the body of Christ that perform important functions. I do wonder, however, whether their contributions are less beneficial to the body of Christ as a whole than they might be were they to practice *under different constraints or through different processes*. To put it a different way, I wonder if we have adopted too readily certain notions of influence, reform, and justice without subjecting such notions to the rigorous evaluation of the Christian mind. In the end, the goal is not to eliminate one group or another, but to ensure that those in positions of influence have "skin in the game."

Accountability as a "Skin in the Game" Sort of Problem

Minimizing upside for prominent pastors, speakers, and writers in a capitalist society is tricky, in part, because any solutions offered seem to have an underlying tone of socialism and a movement toward egalitarianism. While such may seem to be the case, the reality is that an egalitarian impulse is far from what is proposed. It is not so much that wealth, popularity, reputation, and the like need to be redistributed equally amongst the community of faith. To engineer such a redistribution would not actually address the issue of "upside" and "downside," nor would it necessarily improve any individual or collective sense of responsibility. Instead, what is needed to drive a skin-in-the-game sort of accountability is (1) an individual and corporate responsibility for the unity, growth, and general well-being of the body of Christ and all its members and (2) a willingness to understand that the positions we occupy as members of the body are bound up with the body's other members and cannot be advanced as if they have no impact on the church as a whole.

That said, if we are to address the issue of accountability as a "skin in the game" sort of problem, we must have crystal clarity about the church's *telos*…an endpoint with a gravity that compels God's people to act with one accord along diverse trajectories toward the same goal. Without such a *telos*, God's people will, I think, find it quite challenging to move beyond an individual, moral accountability to a skin-in-the-game accountability. Such is the case because to move toward the latter sort of accountability requires more than a checklist of standards applied to the evaluation of individual behavior and the manner in which such behavior impacts individuals in a given situation. Skin-in-the-game accountability does not simply address immoral acts, but evaluates moral acts with reference to a clearly defined *telos*. In this manner, skin-in-the-game accountability calls the various members of the body to do more than simply assert rights or engage in "authorized" behaviors without reflection on how those behaviors impact the rest of the body.

Rather, it calls them to act so as to testify to the reign of God through the building up of a unified community of disciples. It calls them to live under an old command made new "because the darkness is passing away and the true light is already shining" (1 John 2:8). Central to this community of disciples is love for one another expressed in an ongoing (though not perfect; cf. 1 John 2:1) obedience to God's commandments and His command to walk in love (2 John 6). Encoded into the Old and New Testament scriptures (cf. Deut 6:4-5;

Lev 19:18, 34; Matt 22:37-40) and exemplified in the sacrifice of Christ, the commandment to love continues to guide and direct the community of faith and to serve as a sign of the community's authenticity in Christ (1 John 2:9-14). This sort of *telos* requires more of God's people than just avoiding deviant behaviors...it requires a submission of one's whole self to God's agenda.

It is through our submission to God's agenda that we move from having skin in the game to having "soul in the game," to sacrificing our own upside to take on someone else's downside. It is likely that we will be in anguish about how deeply broken the world is. It is important to remember that such anguish derives from a keen sense that the world is not as it should be. This sense is only amplified as we recognize that to follow the commandment of God we may be required to (1) transform our desires and our personal ambitions to more fully align with the workings of God toward the *telos* we share with the rest of the community of faith, (2) surrender our rights and our participation in some of the "good gifts" of God so as to ensure that we do not "destroy the work of God," or (3) curb our messianic impulses which make us less-than patient as we recognize our capacity to help, but choose to wait for God to act. As we come to a fuller understanding of the kingdom by submitting all we are and have to the rule of God, the stark contrast between a life lived with God and a life lived without Him will only become more and more clear.

To suggest that accountability is a skin-in-the-game sort of problem rather than a personal, isolated moral problem is to recognize that our actions (good and bad) have reverberations throughout the community of faith. While this way of framing accountability does not preclude pastors or other Christians from developing a following nationally or internationally, it may raise new questions that seem to be less frequently included in current dialogues. For instance, what connections does the content offered on Christian radio, podcasting or Christian publishing have to the life of local communities of faith? Asking the question in this manner, gets at a crucial point related to the coordination of agendas in local congregations and in the broader body of Christ as a whole. Speakers and authors who create disruptions in local congregations by (a) writing and speaking on a more popular level and (b) writing and speaking on topics that are controversial within the community of faith have the ability to create unnecessary anxieties in local congregations with which local pastors and local communities must deal. Anyone who speaks or writes must consider the potentially negative impact (the creation of downside) their speaking or writing may have, particularly in a digital age.

Thoughts on How Skin-in-the-Game Accountability Might Look

Proposing that accountability within the Christian community might be strengthened by thinking about it in terms of having skin-in-the-game is rather simple. Understanding how such a skin-in-the-game sort of strategy might be implemented is a bit more complicated. Whatever else is entailed, skin-in-the-game accountability encompasses at least individuals and structures, as well as involving reevaluations of the characteristics the Christian community identifies as constitutive of core Christian identity.

If the community of faith were to make the shift to skin-in-the-game accountability, it would be necessary to avoid demonization of those who may currently be experiencing upside with little to no downside. While there is certainly something wrong with the way certain individuals act and with the manner in which we have structured ourselves within the body of Christ, there is no one individual or set of individuals to blame. Making a fundamental shift in the way we think about accountability is not a matter of condemning one group so that another can claim the higher moral ground. Instead, it is an act of realization and recognition that our individual and communal practices are flawed, incomplete, and in need of revision.

Considering the Individual

Before turning to more structural solutions, it is important to note that the most crucial aspect of skin-in-the-game accountability lies with individual Christians. People of influence are not (at least in the context of the church) influential because they have forced their way into a position of power from which they may shape the community of faith according to their will. Instead, those in a position of influence, particularly within a more capitalist and mass media oriented society, have a following. Audiences participate in the process of creating influencers.

This is not to suggest that the often touted power of "word of mouth" is the culprit behind the growth of a particular topic or concept. As Derek Thompson demonstrates, "going viral" is something of a myth that ignores "dark broadcasts" in which the single or small set of established influencers with large audiences who "share" an idea, product, post, video, etc., are forgotten. In other words, "going viral" is often less a function of grass roots, word-of-mouth efforts than it is of unnoticed mechanisms of mass distribution.[290]

As such, individual Christians need to be discerning about the content they choose to consume, the way in which they choose to consume it, and the manner in which such consumption influences their subsequent behavior and thought. There is nothing inherently wrong with mass distribution. Christian authors and speakers whose content is broadly disseminated are not evil or immoral.

There may, however, be a problem when the big voices who gain mind space in the heads of individual Christians through mass distribution channels, cause individual Christians to have a diminished view of those who are in the trenches with them day after day. It becomes a problem when voices abstracted from one's own local community of faith are used to undercut or otherwise discount the wisdom and authority of the God-ordained men and women who oversee with care a local body. The local body still needs to be lead locally even if it is informed nationally and globally.

It is certainly the case that local ministers are also subject to critique. The point is not to elevate the local pastor to the status of saint by demonizing more prominent speakers and authors. Rather, it is to suggest that individual Christians must take care not to mistake (1) familiarity with intimacy or (2) popularity with wisdom. Regarding the former, it is important to understand that those whose thoughts are mass distributed aren't really speaking to individual Christians…at least not in the same way that someone who has a deep knowledge of a particular community might. That's not a bad thing, but it is certainly a distinction worth noting. Instead, mass distributed content speaks to topics that are generally of interest to a wide set of individual Christians (whether such an interest is God-honoring or not). Those who have a broad audience become familiar to us, but there is no real intimacy there. To use an analogy, no matter how often I watch Rocky (I, II, III, IV, V, and Balboa)…I still don't know Sylvester Stallone. There is a difference between familiarity and intimacy.

There is also a difference between popularity and wisdom. If, as Thompson argues, quality is a necessary, but insufficient characteristic for becoming popular, it stands to reason that some of what becomes popular exhibits less quality than what doesn't. If we were to simply take a step back and think about some of the biggest movements, best selling books, or most popular radio programs and podcasts, it seems obvious that popularity is no guarantee of wisdom. For instance, while it might be easy to take pot shots at non-Christian books with sensational titles and edgy content like *The Subtle Art of Not Giving a F*ck*, which appeared in Amazon's Top Ten best sellers list in both 2017 and 2018 and is still in the top 20 in 2019, the dynamics that drive those sales are not so different from those that sustain large radio ministries, fill the seats of mega-churches, and drive the purchase of popular Christian books.

Mass distribution of content makes it feel as though a book or a conversation is important and that the major players in that conversations have their finger on the pulse of something key and core to the Christian situation. While that may be the case in certain instances, it doesn't guarantee it. There are a number of unpopular, low-selling works that contain keen insights that would be crucial to the church. The lack of popularity does not speak to the wisdom contained in the work…it speaks to poor distribution and a lack of interest in the market (among other things). There is a difference between popularity and wisdom.

Individual Christians not only have a stake in working toward skin-in-the-game accountability, they also have some culpability in producing and sustaining the situation in which some experience upside with no downside. It is not so much that individual Christians should abandon any and all mass distributed content. Instead, they should seek to appreciate the gifts God has provided in their local community of faith as well as appreciating the insights of faithful believers with broader reach. Putting the role and value of mass distributed content into proper perspective seems to me to be key to cultivating a grateful and gracious heart that recognizes the unique contributions of the (relatively) unknown, local voices and the more prominent voices alike. Individual Christians would do well to view the "next big thing" promoted on the radio or through a major Christian publisher as, at best, supplemental to the strong, formational relationships forged within the local body of Christ.

Considering Structural Concerns

The tension between structural concerns and personal responsibility is challenging to navigate. Whether Hunter overstates his case in *To Change the World* or not, his work serves to highlight the significance of broader social structures in shaping and maintaining values and behaviors.[291] The way in which we are arranged within society and the manner in which we understand our various relationships have both positive and negative implications. Any arrangement this side of heaven will. Structure matters.

Because structure matters, achieving skin-in-the-game accountability will likely require fundamental changes to the ways in which we structure our relationships within the community of faith and how we think about ministry growth and influence. The good news is that we already have a significant amount of instruction regarding structure in the biblical description of the body of Christ. If, as Piccard argues, "...the purpose of the Church has to do with displaying, embodying, and so manifesting divine wisdom," we have a clear understanding of the *telos* that can guide our thinking concerning the trajectory of God's people and the manner in which individual actors contribute to or detract from that trajectory.[292] In addition, if we also accept that "...seeking after God is fundamentally a pilgrimage in the company of others" and that "...To develop a doctrine of the church from this perspective...implies a critique of those ways of being the Church more in tune with 'steady state' and change-resistant approaches to Church and institutional life," we place the church's flexibility at the core of what it means to be a community of faith.[293]

Working from the purpose of demonstrating divine wisdom and a recognition that the church's fluidity is a fundamental aspect of its character, we can begin to sketch out the necessary components of a skin-in-the-game sort of accountability. Activities of the body as a whole and its individual members may be assessed according to at least three criteria associated with skin-in-the-game accountability: (1) the extent to which a given activity or orientation diminishes the community's capacity to display God's multifaceted wisdom, (2) the extent to which a given activity or orientation denies the community opportunities to situate itself in the world *so as to conform more closely to the image of Christ,* and/or (3) the extent to which an activity or orientation creates upside for an individual or group within the body by creating *unwarranted* downside for other individuals or groups.

While framing the criteria in the negative has its own set of problems, the point of doing so is to recognize that good activities can have negative consequences that may or may not make such activities liabilities to the community of faith. Even if such "good activities" are deemed sufficiently beneficial to continue, identifying the downside they produce for certain members of the body of Christ may offer the crucial insights needed to reduce or eliminate that downside. This approach would not necessarily eliminate good activities that also have negative consequences (it seems to me that if that were the aim, we would have no good activities left to do). Rather, it would recognize that, in a world that is not as it should be, even well-intended, God-honoring actions are incomplete and are often not without negative repercussions for certain members of the body of Christ.

The first and second criteria address activities and orientations that hinder the church from being the church. **Criteria one** includes an issue that I will describe as "over-speaking" within community. Originally, I had considered the labels of "less-heard" and "more-heard" voices within community; however, such terms convey a note of equality that is no less troubling than the phenomenon of "over-speaking." By "over-speaking" I mean that dynamic of discourse whereby influential voices within the community dominate the conversation to the extent that they functionally silence other members of the community with crucial information or perspectives that would allow the community of faith to think differently about a given situation.

"Over-speaking" does not have to do with "giving equal voice to all members at all times" (an egalitarian impulse). To describe "over-speaking" in this fashion neglects the clearly demarcated, God-given positions and giftings of the individual members of the body. God's arrangement of His diverse people with a multiplicity of gifts will surely produce a multiplicity of viewpoints. In the ongoing life of the church, a given viewpoint may be more or less appropriate at a given time. Over-speaking would deny viewpoints appropriate to a given situation by allowing voices or sets of voices within the body to seep out of their realm of responsibility to diminish the volume of other voices.

Think of "over-speaking" as an instance in which the arms and hands atrophy because the feet and legs are used for activities the arms and hands should rightly be doing (e.g. feeding oneself, typing, etc.). It is not so much that the feet and legs do not have a role in the body. Rather, it is that the hands and arms also have a role and when that role is denied, the body becomes less whole.

Take, for instance, a church that holds to the complementarian position precluding women from serving as elders. While such a theological position is not problematic on its face, the resulting structures and procedures have the potential to obscure female perspectives from the deliberations of all-male elder boards.[294] The complementarian position does not prohibit male elders from engaging women and listening to their unique, God-given perspective on matters concerning the church. However, engagement with women in the congregation with the intention of better understanding their perspectives and factoring such perspectives into decision making is not necessarily structured into every all-male elder board. The theological position does not preclude engagement with the perspectives and concerns of women, but, as the theological position is structured into the practice of the church, the theological position can be distorted and perverted by structures and procedures that do not guard against over-speaking.

Criteria two addresses the position of the church in the world. This criteria does not advantage those who prefer the status quo or those who advocate for change. Instead, this criteria is intended to root the church's discernment in history…to help the church remember that what it means to be faithful may take on different forms at different times. Understanding how to be a community of faith at a given point in history requires adaptation, yet such adaptation cannot proceed without a deep, enduring sense of history. We have to understand why the faithful men and women of the past set up the institutions they did.

As G.K. Chesterton notes,

> "…nobody has any business to destroy a social institution until he has really seen it as an historical institution. If he knows how it arose, and what purposes it was supposed to serve, he may really be able to say that they were bad purposes, or that they have since become bad purposes, or that they are purposes which are no longer served. But if he simply stares at the thing as a senseless monstrosity that has somehow sprung up in his path, it is he and not the traditionalist who is suffering from an illusion."[295]

The point is not that the status quo is always superior, but that change is not an activity to be engaged in lightly. As a friend of mine once told me, all change results in loss. Our job is not to prevent change, but to understand deeply the loss we will suffer. To some degree, deciding to change is a decision that what is lost through change is less valuable than what is gained.

While change should not be entered into lightly, our communities must be diligent to avoid sustaining practices that preclude the interrogation of the status quo. If we take seriously G.K. Chesterton's historical criteria, we must remain open to the idea that our various "social institutions" may testify to Christ less faithfully within a new era and/or be less intelligible within a different historical matrix. The historical criteria Chesterton describes suggests that certain social institutions may "age out" as the wheels of history continue to turn.

Even as we learn from faithful men and women of the past, we cannot be naïve to our situation in the present. As a believing community, we must certainly engage in the task of preserving the faith we have been taught (2 Tim 2:2), yet we do so within unique historical circumstances that will often require us to rethink the manner in which we understand our faith. No generation is immune to the influence of frameworks that condition the manner in which the world is viewed. As Johann Huizinga notes, "Every man renders account to himself of the past in accordance with the standards which his education and *Weltanschauung* [worldview] lead him to adopt."[296]

In the end, the second criteria is not intended to slant the church toward change, but toward conformity to the image of Christ. The process of conformity is not achieved through a dogged unwillingness to change or through the flippant abandonment of long-held traditions. Instead, it is accomplished as we surrender our agendas and preferences…past and present…to God's agenda. The second criteria is a caution against becoming too afraid or too stubborn to subject our past to scrutiny or too cavalier in our willingness to chart a new course. It is a call to patient, sustained dialogue that is neither callous to the various ways in which the world is not as it should be, nor given to unreflective, knee-jerk decision-making that becomes too narrowly focused on a particular problem and dismisses strong theological reasoning.

The **third criteria** returns to a common theme running throughout this essay: unwarranted downside. There are certainly cases in which downside is warranted. Our actions have consequences. Yet, when we look at the body of Christ and realize that some of the downside certain members experience is the direct or indirect result of actions that produce upside for others who have little to no downside, we cannot sit on our hands and assume that everything should continue as normal. While uniformity is not a Christian goal, caring for one another…loving one another…is. As such, actions that produce upside for one party and downside for another need to be subjected to deep discernment with the goal of retaining the unity of the body and testifying to Christ by the way we love one another.

Guiding Convictions for Skin-in-the-Game Accountability

Moving beyond evaluative criteria, we must now turn to some of the underlying convictions necessary to accomplish skin-in-the-game accountability in a more organic, proactive fashion. As we understand differently who we are as individuals in Christ and who we are as a community of faith, we may well find that new questions arise that will lead us more naturally toward skin-in-the-game accountability. Such orientations are available in the scriptures though they are not the themes that dominate our conversations within the Christian community. The following three convictions are surely only three among a host of others needed to make skin-in-the-game accountability a more natural part of Christian discourse. At a bare minimum, these three convictions offer the potential for a structure that more fully recognizes the ongoing work of God in community.

<u>Conviction 1: Reciprocity is conditioned upon the ongoing willingness of the collective body and its individual members to discern and respect the God-given roles, capacities, and limitations of the various members of Christ's body.</u>

Reciprocity of the sort that Paul reflects in Romans 1:11-12 is not a matter of false humility. It is the recognition that the community of faith has been brought together for the mutual benefit of each member. While we no longer choose our leaders or make key decisions by lot, practicing the radical act of reciprocity while respecting the God-given gifts and capacities of those whom God has given to the body reflects a regard for God's wisdom and trust in his ongoing activities similar to that required to choose leaders by casting lots.

Reciprocity is the fundamental means by which we demonstrate our gratitude for God's provision of difference within community. We acknowledge both what we and others offer the community as a wise act of divine ordering on which we cannot improve. In allowing ourselves to remain open to the possibility that the other members within our community have something to add to our lives, we rightly position ourselves. We are not overly or falsely humble, but reveal ourselves to be individuals who trust deeply that God has gifted us to make specific contributions to the assembly while leaving us with specific limitations (areas in which we are incomplete) that allow us to benefit from other members of the community.

The conviction that we can all benefit from one another highlights the necessity of each individual member of the body of Christ. Recognizing reciprocity cultivates a sense that what appears to be good only for me (or those like me) may not actually be good for me (or those like me). Reciprocity changes the calculus of Christian activity because we can no longer simply attend to what is good for "me," but must consider how our actions are good for the community as a whole. In other words, skin-in-the-game accountability recognizes reciprocity in so much as individual or group activity is evaluated, in part, on its potential to help the church be the church.

<u>Conviction 2: Impartiality is a crucial practice within the community of faith for which multiple sorts of difference (e.g. socio-cultural, ethnic, gender-based, and generational) are intrinsic.</u>

The New Testament speaks of partiality beyond the legal realm. As Peter and Paul note, God shows no partiality (Acts 10:34; Rom 2:11; Gal 2:6; Eph 6:9). Paul and James also give direction urging impartiality in judgment and discernment (1 Tim 5:21; James 2:1-9). In the Old Testament, impartiality is most often discussed in judicial contexts. The poor, widow, and orphan are not to be treated unfairly so that inappropriate preference may be given to the rich and powerful (Exod 23:2, 6; Deut 1:17; 10:17; 16:19; Prov 28:21). At the same time, the poor are not to be given preferential treatment because of their lowly position (Exod 23:3; Lev 19:15; Deut 1:17).

Rather, the goal is a righteous discernment uninfluenced by bribes or intimidation on the one hand or, presumably, sentimentality or moral outrage on the other. The rich are not always wrong, nor are the poor deserving of unwarranted judgment simply because of their circumstances. Impartiality entails a willingness to set aside one's own upside and agenda in order to discern faithfully what is right and just. While we may have an affinity with one group or benefit by one story as opposed to another, "affinity" and "benefit" are not "justice" and "righteousness."

Impartiality requires us to do more than hold an opinion…we must set aside our own preconceived notions and take on the burden of making right judgments even when such judgments may result in a downside for us or those we care about. Skin-in-the-game accountability demands impartial judgments rather than the sort of advocacy and interest that might appear expedient and, perhaps necessary, to right some wrong in the world. Those with skin-in-the-game in the church recognize that expediency may not benefit the community of faith or convey the character of God. Impartiality often calls those with skin-in-the-game to take longer and harder roads towards change when other more easily navigable paths are available.

<u>Conviction 3: Misplaced Loyalty denies the cross its proper, unifying function within the body of Christ.</u>

In 1 Corinthians, Paul urges the Corinthians to avoid divisions and to "be united in the same mind an the same judgment" (1:10). The divisions that were cropping up in Corinth as people chose their preferred ministry was incommensurate with the Christian faith because Christ cannot be divided (1:13). Human ministers do not carry the weight of the cross of Christ, nor

should that inspire or accept the sort of loyalty that masks the cross from view. Herein lies the primary problem Paul appears to address in 1 Corinthians, artful speech is no substitute for the cross. As Schriener notes, "When people exalt ministers and their speaking skills and abilities, the significance of the cross has been forgotten…those who proclaim and preach must beware lest they draw attention to themselves instead of the cross of Christ."[297]

As our allegiances to a particular individual or group create factions by reinforcing a sub-group identity as the superior identity within the body of Christ we (a) grant certain individuals or groups (e.g. denominations) a status they can never actually attain and (b) pervert the gospel by denying the cross of Christ its unifying function.[298] The church is Christ's body…it is not divided. Loyalties that subsume our in-Christ identity under some other identity or attempt to legitimize some sub-group identity as somehow synonymous with or representative of our in-Christ identity are misplaced and detrimental to the community of faith.

Conclusion

Whatever else may be said about accountability (and there is much more than could be said), it is rooted in our "in-Christ" identity. We are not isolated members of the body of Christ, but interconnected members contributing to the overall well-being of the body. Considering accountability from the perspective of having skin-in-the-game offers one way forward in changing the framework through which the Christian community might re-consider its communal life. While there certainly remains a need for personal accountability and moral behavior, we must recast our discussion of accountability to reflect our life in community with one another.

10 Theology As Path Dependent

Introduction

Theology is path dependent. It doesn't just matter where you end up…it matters how you get there. After more than two decades of being committed to theology and theological education, it seems clear to me that God's people (myself included) are too quick to dismiss the path dependent nature of theology. In our quest to ensure adherence to specific doctrinal positions, to participate in the mission of God by making disciples, to fix what is wrong with the world, or to preserve some idea of Christian culture, we are willing to minimize God when we should be making much of Him. We place our trust in programs and processes keeping God involved…but at arm's length. We want Him to take pleasure in what we've accomplished when what He wants is for us to participate in what He is accomplishing.

Cultivating a Christian mind requires a recognition of theology's path dependent nature…we cannot elevate right doctrines or "Christian culture" to the level of a "master-signifier…which retroactively determines"[299] the meanings of other non-master signifiers. It seems to me that some of what we have become so accustomed to defending so vehemently are the exact fetishes of the faith that have led us away from God and toward a less-than comprehensive (and comprehensible) witness.

Utilizing Žižek's concept of "master-signifier," Fitch identified the inerrant Bible, the decision for Christ, and the Christian nation as examples of master-signifiers that have contributed to a diminished form of Christianity. As Fitch notes, "We get a view of just how much we have lost the core of our faith in the process of defending a high view of Scripture, a conversionist cross-centered salvation, and an activist engagement with culture for the gospel."[300] He goes on to suggest, "…in themselves (I would argue) these commitments are crucial to our life as evangelicals and must be preserved. Yet before we can reclaim these beliefs, a space must be opened up whereby we see the emptiness behind the ways we have practiced them as a way of life."[301]

It would seem that we have become overly focused (obsessed) with certain tenants of the faith…we have created a façade that allows us to simplify and manage our individual and collective lives. Unfortunately, this façade has also hidden from view the realities of God's kingdom and the necessity of having more than right belief. After all, as James asserts, "…someone will say, 'You have faith and I have works.' Show me your faith apart from your works, and I will show you my faith by my works. You believe that God is one; you do well. Even the demons believe—and shudder!" (James 2:18-19).

The point is not to question the veracity of confession or to suggest that no one who confesses "Jesus is Lord" really means it. Rather, the point is to recall that our faith is of a certain sort…it is not mere assent, but a commitment to a God-established order of things manifested in the comprehensive testimony of the individual Christian and the collective community of faith. Right doctrine is surely necessary, but not sufficient to cultivate comprehensive Christian testimony. We must also find it in our hearts to lament instead of blame, cry to God for justice rather than taking on the mantle of judge, jury, and executioner, correct our sisters and brothers lovingly, and discipline ourselves to act so as to promote the peace and purity of the body.

It is crucial that we move away from a God-in-man's-world to a man-in-God's-world perspective. To develop a Christian mind we have to find the space in which we can participate with God…a space that lies somewhere on the spectrum between an overly spiritual reasoning that justifies our agendas and preferences and a messianic complex in which we engage in heavy-handed interventions to remake the world in our own image. Avoiding these two tendencies demands a different cadence of living that understands the differences between outcome and process…between the benefits of bing formed by God's process as opposed to forcing the "right" result without submitting to the transformative work of God.

This way of construing the matter begs the question of what it might look like for the church to find a space in which we can participate with God rather than involving Him (or attempting to involve Him) in our own agendas. How might we go about doing more than justifying our activities based solely on the criteria that they are not biblical prohibited or are explicitly authorized in scripture? At what point do the concessions we make to pursue a given organizational mission do a disservice to the body of Christ? To what extent are we contributing to agendas that run counter to the Kingdom of God? Such questions resist hard and fast answers, yet, if we are to begin answering any of them, we must reckon with at least two key areas: (1) our (mis)calculation of the worst case scenarios and (2) our seeming willingness to be distracted from dealing with root causes..

What's the Worst that Could Happen? Avoiding the Wrong Worst Case Scenario

In *Braveheart*, Robert the Bruce becomes entangled in his father's plot to put Robert on the throne of Scotland. His father convinces Robert that to serve his family and Scotland, he must betray William Wallace by handing him over to the King of England. Robert ultimately helps Wallace escape, but not until Robert's betrayal is made known. In a powerful scene, Robert confronts his father:

> **Robert's Father:** "Son, we must have alliance with England to prevail here. You achieved that. You saved your family…increased your land. In time you will have all the power in England."
>
> **Robert:** "Lands, titles, men, power—nothing."

Robert's Father: "Nothing?"

Robert: "I have nothing. Men fight for me because if they do not, I throw them off my land and I starve their wives and their children. Those men who bled the ground red at Falkirk…they fought for William Wallace and he fights for something that I've never had. And I took it from him when I betrayed him, and I saw it on his face in the battlefield and its tearing me apart!

Robert's Father: Well, all men betray…all lose heart.

Robert: I don't want to lose heart! I want to believe…as he does. I will never be on the wrong side again."[302]

In a moment of perfect clarity, Robert the Bruce recognizes that his betrayal was intended to stave off the wrong worst case scenario. He allowed himself to believe that compromising who he was…giving up his integrity…in order to save his family and achieve the thrown was worth it. Losing ground with England, fighting what appeared to be a losing battle against "Longshanks," and, ultimately, putting the people of Scotland at risk seemed like the worst case scenario…but it wasn't. Instead, he realizes the worst case scenario: he gives himself over to a set of actions that compromise his heart and diminish his integrity.

Too often we miscalculate the worst case scenario because we are looking at the outcome, not the process we will ultimately have to take in getting to that outcome. In *Braveheart*, Robert the Bruce becomes convinced that sitting on Scotland's throne, allying with England, and giving the people of Scotland some form of peace is an end that justifies any means. Once the ends justifies the means, we run the risk of forgetting that the worst case scenario is less about the outcome and more about who we demonstrate ourselves to be as we achieve (or fail to achieve) that outcome.

While Robert the Bruce's moral lapse was quite dramatic, my guess is that most times we lose heart through a process akin to erosion. We slowly slowly slough off layer after layer not noticing the longer-term consequences of the small compromises we make in order to achieve some desired outcome. For members of the body of Christ (and the body of Christ as a whole), the worst case scenario is not some epic failure, but successes achieved at the expense of character.

Our character becomes "up for grabs" when we buy-in to the false belief that getting there can be separated from how we get there...when we elevate the outcome over the process. In other words, we adopt a mentality in which the ends justifies the means. Want to keep that seven-figure donor happy, you better make the changes he wants? Interested in shutting down a social media storm and getting that annoying blogger to leave you alone? Easy, just make a call that undercuts you leadership and staff. Do what is expedient and not wrong...don't worry so much about doing what is right.

This last distinction...between what is "not wrong" and what is right...is an important one because the former is generally employed when doing what is right gets too difficult, too costly. Doing what is "not wrong" speaks to a choice that does not violate any specific moral or cultural norm, but is actually an easy, whitewashed decision that has only the appearance righteousness. No one will be called out as being publicly disqualified for this sort of decision...some might even applaud those who make them and see it as a move in the right direction. In reality, however, doing what is "not wrong" does a different sort of damage to the community of faith by blinding us to a reality from which we should be attempting to escape or to which we should be standing in opposition. In short, they are spineless, cowardly decisions that no more reflect the character of God than the "heinous" acts "not wrong" decisions are so often constructed to address.

Too often such choices are the fruit of a decision-making tradition in which hard decisions are never made, so, when one's hand is forced one's tradition results in an improvisation toward ease, self-preservation, and being "not wrong." Wells describes this dynamic in a more aspirational tone noting,

"The Bible is not so much a script that the church learns and performs as it is a training school that shapes the habits and practices of a community. This community learns to take the right things for granted, and on the basis of this faithfulness, it trusts itself to improvise within its tradition. Improvisation means a community formed in the right habits of trusting itself to embody its tradition in new and often challenging circumstances; and this is exactly what the church is called to do."[303]

While I would not deny the positive dynamic that Wells highlights, traditions have the ability to form people in less-positive ways as well. Their improvisations are not aimed at righteousness, but at stability and status quo.

In order to avoid confusion, it must be noted that doing what is "not wrong" is different than having what is right result in negative consequences for others. Doing what is right is not always popular, nor will it always result in success. Rather, doing what is right is a choice for integrity despite consequences, whereas choosing what is "not wrong" is a choice for pleasing a powerful constituency or preserving what could be lost. It is a subtle form of "naïve intervention," or a "need to 'do something'" that results in harm.[304] Instead of allowing an organization, process, or system to feel the strain of some external pressure so that it can either be refined and strengthened or shattered and ended.

Making a "not wrong" decision greatly increases the chances of realizing the worst case scenario…of elevating ends over means and compromising character for outcomes. Considering that to be a theologian is "to seek, speak, and show understanding of what God was doing in Christ for the sake of the world," Christians do not get to take a break from being theologians. We walk our paths as theologians constantly learning, proclaiming, and embodying our testimony. In large part, theology is path dependent because theology is not confined to the pages of a systematic theology textbook, but comes to life as we engage a fallen world determined to demonstrate the sort of character a life with God produces and sustains.

Distracted

In his book entitled *Leadership without Easy Answers*, Heifetz notes, "…getting people to clarify what matters most, in what balance, with what trade-offs, becomes a central task…Strategy begins with asking: Which stakeholders have to adjust their ways to make progress on this problem? How can one sequence the issues or strengthen the bonds that join the stakeholders together as a community of interests so that they withstand the stresses of problem-solving?"[305] They also note that a certain sort of leadership is necessary to face adaptive challenges, or those "that demand innovation and learning."[306] It is the sort of leadership "that will challenge us to face problems for which there are no simple, painless solutions—problems that require us to learn new ways."[307]

The manner of leadership we normally look for is the sort that "can make hard problems simple," but this sort of leadership cannot help us make "changes in our attitudes, behavior and values."[308] In short, we like for leadership to offer the façade of solutions…to comfort us that there is a way forward that will not require much effort or change on our part. We want someone else to solve our problems for us. To the extent that we continue to define leadership in terms of "influencing the community to follow the leader's vision" rather than "influencing the community to face its problems," we will, it seems to me, be more prone to distraction…to ignoring the deeper problems facing our community.

If, as Heifetz argues, our conception of leadership is keeping us from addressing "adaptive problems," that same conception of leadership feeds distraction. Whatever impact the sheer volume of beeps and pings that come across our mobile devices have on our attention, perhaps the most deceptive culprit fueling our distraction comes from the leaders and influencer we listen to most intently. While looking to leaders to solve our problems is wrongheaded, allowing leaders to define our problems is the more severe pathology.

Arguably, prominent Christian leaders and influencers point to issues like abortion, intersectionality, social justice, and the roles of women in the church as problems…the watershed issues of the Christian community today. The solution to these problems most often includes political action where we rally around one candidate or proposition in the hopes that America will eventually turn back to the moral purpose on which our nation was founded.[309] It is not that the state of the Union is not important. There is plenty of reason to attend to the issues concerning our nation. Yet, it would seem that we have, in certain circles, decided that the Christian community is a political and selectively moral community rather than a theological community. It is time for the Christian community to recognize that the problems we face are, at root, theological rather than moral or political, yet we often allow the moral and political concerns of the day to distract us from our fuller theological task.

Take, for instance, homosexuality. The Bible is quite clear that homosexual activities are incommensurate with the kingdom of God. Add concerns that same sex marriage will tear the social fabric of our country apart to the Bible's various prohibitions and it starts to feel like if we don't fight back against the homosexual lobby, we will not only be compromising our faith, but allowing America to go to hell in a hand basket. Yet, when looking at certain passages, like 1 Corinthians 6:9-10, in which Paul notes that "men who practice homosexuality" will not "…inherit the kingdom of God," we have a tendency to gloss over some of the other groups listed. Where, for instance, is the public outcry (or the outcry within the church) against "the greedy"? Arguably this group is just as pernicious and problematic…just as damaging to the social fabric…as "men who practice homosexuality." It seems that greed, at least to a certain degree, is a far more acceptable "white collar crime." It is, unlike homosexuality, something tolerable within limits.

What of "revilers" or "thieves" or "adulterers" or the "sexually immoral"? Presumably the inclusion of these categories in Paul's list in 1 Corinthians means that these patterns of activity are incommensurate with the Christian life. As Thiselton puts it, "The new life is no longer characterized by the practice of evil, habitual drunkenness, the practice of verbal abuse, or the exploitation of others…These are patterns of life, not isolated sins."[310] Despite the inclusion of a category like "revilers," we seem content to allow some within the Christian community to engage in a pattern of "verbal abuse" that degrades, diminishes, or dismisses other members of the body of Christ. While we may express our disappointment over the language used by certain prominent members of our community, such concerns don't seem to rise to the level of more politically oriented issues despite the biblical emphasis on speech and the tongue (Prov 6:17; 10:20, 31; 12:18; Jer 9:3, 5; Micah 6:12; Zeph 3:13; Rom 3:13; James 1:26; 3:5-8; 1 Pet 3:10).

Why is it that some sins have been elevated while others seem to go relatively unaddressed? We've been distracted. We have decided to let our leaders shoulder the responsibility for making the church work and have effectively absolved ourselves from facing problems that challenge our community. They represent us but in a way that minimizes our role in the overall functioning of the community of faith. Our fundamental misunderstanding of leadership or our unwillingness to accept leaders who will call us to account has created a situation in which we can focus our attention on venerating leaders who solve our problems and dismissing those who can't (or won't).

The point is not to deny the significance of any particular sin, nor is it to say that if we aren't going to address all of the items in Paul's list, we shouldn't address any of them. Rather, the point is that our overemphasis on certain sins is distracting us…diverting our attention…from deeper theological problems within our own community. Distraction, however, is not the problem…the problem is one of community. As a community, we seem to be either unwilling or incapable of cultivating the sort of leadership capable of convincing us to face our real problems. In other words, our distraction is, to one degree or another, our own choice because, as Hauerwas rightly notes, "Many of the proposals about leadership are quite perverse, exactly because it gives the impression that you know what leadership is abstracted from communities that make leadership possible."[311]

Our distractions, particularly in an overemphasis on a particular sin or political crisis, suggest that we have, on some basic level, misunderstood who we are in Christ. It is not so much that we should ignore issues and problems as they arise. For instance, at the time of writing the scandal du jour is related to the treatment of women in the Southern Baptist church and the various accusations and admissions that appear to be revealing that women have been subjected to inappropriate behavior on a more systemic scale. While those who have engaged in such behavior should certainly be held accountable, it is not clear that, beyond removing or otherwise responding to individual concerns, we as a community have a forum to critically consider what needs to change so that sexually inappropriate behavior and the abuse of power do not become systemic problems in the future. The social media storm prompts some changes, but doesn't (or hasn't yet) offered the sort of sustained energy or purpose to make system-wide changes, to reorient attitudes and behaviors that have developed through misconceptions concerning certain theological perspectives, or to reckon with what happens when social media pressure gets it wrong.

While it is not solely a matter of distraction that has led us astray, distraction contributes to our ongoing dysfunctions by keeping us from getting down to the deeper concerns plaguing our community. To put it another way, distractions keep us focused on important symptoms at the expense of solving for an underlying root cause. It is certainly true that sin is that underlying root cause, but of what sort? What underlying dynamics or false beliefs are sustaining the habits of thought and behavior by which we contribute to the dysfunction, delusion, and depravity of the fallen world in which we live? Distraction is not, in my estimation, the root cause, but a closely related symptom and a key part of the underlying dynamics that keep us from addressing our deeper issues.

Distraction leads us to react and respond. It cultivates a sense of urgency…a sense that if we do not act, we will surrender ground that we cannot win back. If only we can make it through this next challenge, defend this next position, and wether this next storm, all will be well. Unfortunately, the "next" challenge, position, and storm is always followed by another. The battles don't stop, but at some point what we are fighting for becomes less and less clear. In part, that is because the distractions begin to become our reality. Unfortunately, the distractions have no particular theological substance. Fighting to fend off this group or that group, rallying around a given piece of legislation, or combatting a pernicious trend of activities in the church are not sinful activities, but when they do not emanate from a more centered theological core, they run the risk of becoming human quests devoid of God. It seems to me that there is a way for us to lose sight of God in the battle…for the battle itself to become a distraction that causes us to forget God.

Conclusion

I began this essay with a relatively simple statement: theology is path dependent. The ends do not justify the means. Instead, the means are ends in and of themselves because the way we are in the world is an expression of our theology. Our theology is not conveyed in our successes or our failures. It is conveyed through our faithfulness, through our willingness to "lose" because we are committed to following God, and through our unyielding submission to the Holy Spirit and the word of God. Anything that distracts from those aims…that substitutes our agenda for God's…becomes a space ripe for theological distortion, for division, and, ultimately, for a less-than faithful testimony to God in the world.

11 Conclusion

When I started these essays, I was angry. I had just been through what I hope is the worst year of my professional life. I felt betrayed, foolish, and vulnerable. I wanted to retaliate. That rather difficult year as an academic dean was full of hard decisions, internal and external accusations, and second-guessing of decisions. It produced in me a sense of frustration, distrust, anger, and injustice. Several initial drafts of the essays in this volume were too sarcastic, cynical, and biting to be characterized as Christian. As I wrote (and rewrote) each essay, I found myself becoming less angry and more concerned with conveying my thoughts in a way that was honoring to God. I wanted to articulate myself in a manner that showed reverence for God and a healthy respect for those God has positioned in this world.

During my final year as an academic dean at Moody Bible Institute (MBI), I learned what it means to face impossible choices. As I and several of my colleagues waded into grey areas and sought to be prayerful and wise as we dealt with a host of ambiguities, others inside and outside of MBI did what only those who do not shoulder the weight of responsibility that comes with leadership can: they simplified the challenges we were facing until there were no areas of grey left…only black or white. More than that, I watched as those who saw only a small sliver of evidence or refused to allow for different perspectives on the broader situation demonize the work of good women and men, make accusations about their character and competence, and seek to reform through coercion rather than transform through serious analysis.

Our current media environment isn't likely to change in the foreseeable future. Fortunately, it isn't our media environment that is the problem. We are. The media to which we currently have access allows us opportunities for dignified, imaginative, and artistic expression that the past media outlets constrained as they were by space, time, and cost simply could not provide. They also allow us the opportunity for reactionary, harsh, under-informed (or misinformed) expression that diminishes others and divides the body of Christ.

It will be up to individual Christians and the body of Christ as a whole to resist the urge to adopt social media practices incommensurate with our "in Christ" identity. More than use of media, we must begin to broaden our scope of vision to consider how best to organize ourselves and to interact with one another as citizens of a heavenly polis responsible to and for one another. Perhaps most important of all, we must develop space for theological thought where the Christian mind can thrive. We need a space to have the sort of slow, deliberate dialogues that reflect our deep conviction that discerning the Spirit is crucial to offering faithful testimony.

The Christian mind is not, I fear, something we will develop organically, that is, without effort and intention. It will require far more of us than the oft cited disciplines of prayer, bible reading, and community. These disciplines are essential, but not likely sufficient to represent the range of practices necessary to develop as disciples in a world of distractions. Like anyone who has ever tried to lose weight can attest, you not only have to attend to the food you eat, but also to the food you keep in the house. A cupboard full of potato chips, cookies, and other goodies will often be too much to resist. Eliminating those foods from the environment is often the best first step toward more healthy eating.

In a similar way, to develop a Christian mind, we are going to need to purge our cupboards of those books, blog posts, Tweets, PR releases, sermons, or news stories that deter the community of faith from cultivating a comprehensive theological vision of reality. We must begin to ask ourselves whether the conversations and communities of which we are a part are hindering us from knowing God more deeply. To develop a Christian mind we must have the courage to ask and answer hard questions about ourselves and the body of Christ more broadly. Perhaps the most basic, yet essential, question is this: How is it that we have, in the midst of our agendas, strategies, moral outrage, and legitimate concerns, fashioned God into a deity of our own making so that He looks increasingly like us rather than us being transformed to look increasingly like Him? God, give us the courage to be women and men who refuse to make You in our image, but surrender ourselves to being formed into Your's.

Acknowledgments

First and foremost, I would like to acknowledge my wife Kim for her support, patience, and insight throughout this project. I'm thankful for my kids (Judah, Savanah, and Scarlett) who provided fun and levity…the right sort of distractions…keeping me from being overly focused on this work.

Elizabeth and Brian have been faithful conversation partners, as well as offering encouragement and friendship through a challenging year and through the challenges of writing. Thanks also to John who took the time to read an initial manuscript and make comments that have strengthened this work.

I'd also like to thank my extended family who have given me the time needed to write and think by helping with our biological and foster children.

I'm grateful to all of those who have read my blog, which I've often used as a testing ground to clarify my thoughts on a variety of issues. I'm particularly grateful to those who have made comments in-person or online and urged me to keep writing.

I have also been blessed to be a part of two organizations while writing this book. The first is Moody Center, which has provided the space for me to rediscover what it means for an organization to pursue God. Thanks to Emmitt Mitchell and the Moody Center board for giving me a home after higher ed. The second is Right on Mission where I was first introduced to the concept of the Christian Mind. Thanks to Sarah Sumner and the rest of the Right on Mission team for affording me the opportunity to teach Developing a Christian Mind.

Last, but by no means least, I want to acknowledge God. Whether this book sells one copy (thanks mom!) or 1,000,000, God has formed and shaped the way I think and act through the process of writing. I'm different now than I was when I started writing this set of essays a little more than a year ago. God has…as always…shown Himself faithful

Endnotes

[1] Here it is worth noting the paradigm used by Ravi Zacharias in which the "four inescapable questions...dealing with origin, meaning, morality, and desitiny" form and shape the manner in which we understand the world around us. These questions, when answered from a Christian perspective provide a powerful guiding framework for the way in which Christian interact with God and His creation. See Ravi Zacharias, *Can Man Live Without God* (Nashville: W Pinlishing Group, 1994).

[2] Charles Taylor, *Modern Social Imaginaries*, (Durham: Duke University Press, 2004), 83.

[3] The phrase "Christian mind" is one borrowed from Harry Blamires who bemoans the loss of a truly Christian mind "...a mind trained, informed, equipped to handle data of secular controversy with a framework of reference which is constructed of Christian presuppositions" which can engage in Christian thinking, dialogue and action. See Harry Blamires, *The Christian Mind: How Should a Christian Think?* (London: S.P.C.K., 1963), 43.

[4] Jennings offers what is likely the most sustained argument of the importance of place noting at one point "the deepest theological distortion taking place is that the earth, the ground, spaces, and places are being removed as living organizers of identity and as facilitators of identity" (39). See Willie James Jennings, *The Christian Imagination: Theology and the Origins of Race* (New Haven: Yale University Press, 2010).

[5] While we have a number of fantastic resources from past Christian authors, we have not been as diligent in investigating and incorporating the whole of the church's history and discourse. Western European authors have, to a large degree, shaped the academic theological discourse and, thus, much of the church's modern discourse. These theological resources are an invaluable part of our complex, historical memory, but do not constitute the full account of worldwide Christianity. For an excellent example of the potential available global Christian history, see Justo L. Gonzalez, *The Changing Shape of Church History* (St. Louis: Chalice, 2002).

[6] Jeffrey K. Olick, *The Politics of Regret: On Collective Memory and Historical Responsibility* (New York: Routledge, 2007), 86.

[7] Richard E. Averbeck, *God, People, and the Bible: The Relationship between Illumination and Biblical Scholarship* (Dallas: Biblical Studies, 2005), 148-149.

[8] Stanley Hauerwas, *The Work of Theology* (Grand Rapids: Eerdmans, 2015), 39.

[9] Kevin J. Vanhoozer and Owen Strachan, *The Pastor as Public Theologian: Reclaiming a Lost Vision* (Grand Rapids: Baker, 2015), 17.

[10] Concerning the question of character versus credentials see the fascinating analysis of various secular thinkers and their capacity to chart a course for human affairs in Paul Johnson, *Intellectuals: From Marx and Tolstoy to Sartre and Chomsky* (New York:

HarperCollins, 2007). Concerning popularity, note Thompson's comment regarding the spread of popular music: "In the twentieth century, most pop songs became popular because they played on the radio or on other mass media broadcasts again and again…In the nineteenth century, however, songs by famous composers may have hopped between concert halls, but there was no adequate technology to quickly move a song around the globe" (Derek Thompson, *Hit Makers: The Science of Popularity in an Age of Distraction* [New York: Penguin, 2017], 4).

[11] If, as Huizinga notes, "Every man renders account to himself of the past in accordance with the standards which his education and *Weltanschauung* [worldview] lead him to adopt," it is clear that as new education and perspectives on the world arise, old accounts of the past (and present) will prove themselves incomplete (Johann Huizinga, "A Definition of the Concept of History," in *Philosophy and History: Essays Presented to Ernst Cassier* [ed. R. Klibansky and H. J. Paton; New York: Harper and Row, 1963], 6). The unfinished nature of the accounts rendered, however, does not necessarily require dismissal or demonization, but supplementation and revision.

[12] Kevin J. Vanhoozer, *The Drama of Doctrine: A Canonical Linguistic Approach to Christian Theology* (Louisville: Westminster John Knox, 2005), 234.

[13] Taylor, *Modern Social Imaginaries*, 23.

[14] Oliver O'Donovan, *The Desire of the Nation's: Rediscovering the Roots of Political Theology* (Cambridge: Cambridge University Press, 1996), 80.

[15] This concept is similar to that described by O'Donovan regarding Christian freedom: "Thus, Christian freedom, given by the Holy Spirit, allows man to make moral responses creatively…As a moral agent in history he has to interpret new situations, plumbing their meanings and declaring them by his decision. This kind of authority is not a challenge to the authority of God; it is a restoration of Adam's lordship in the natural order…" (Oliver O'Donovan, *Resurrection and Moral Order: An Outline for Evangelical Ethics* [Grand Rapids: Eerdmans, 1994], 24).

[16] Claude Welch, *The Reality of the Church* (New York: Charles Scribner's Sons, 1958), 121.

[17] Jeffrey K. Olick, "Collective Memory and Cultural Constraint: Holocaust Myth and Rationality in German Politics," *American Sociological Review* 62 (1997): 934.

[18] See James H. Cone, *The Cross and the Lynching Tree* (Maryknoll: Orbis, 2011) and Justo L. González, *Mañana: Christian Theology from a Hispanic Perspective* (Nashville: Abingdon, 1990).

[19] C. A. J. Coady, *Testimony: A Philosophical Study* (Oxford: Clarendon, 1992), 52.

[20] See the discussion of doctrine as a means of social demarcation in Alister E. McGrath, *The Genesis of Doctrine: A Study in the Foundation of Doctrinal Criticism* (Grand Rapids: Eerdmans, 1990), 37-52.

[21] There is good reason to exercise caution with regard to the standards of academia and journalism. O'Keefe highlights some of the challenges associated with mainstream media, which, he argues, begins with a rather troubling orientation to the public. He advocates for and practices a sort of journalism that "…stands in stark contrast to the de facto vision of the mainstream media that detest a free people…They prefer to spoon-feed select information and final conclusions to the public rather than to provide individuals the raw information required to reach conclusions on their own. Instead of 'news,' their audiences get relentless punditry, editorializing, and politically loaded programming" (James O'Keefe, *American Pravda: My Fight for Truth in the Era of Fake News* [New York: St. Martin's, 2018], 13-14). Academia does not seem to be fairing much better. The range of opinions regarding why the academy has become less and less effective ranges from concerns about the corporatization of education to the turn toward identity politics and the loss of open academic discourse. For the latter, see Sean Stevens, "The Skeptics Are Wrong Part 2: Speech Culture on Campus is Changing," Heterodox Academy, April 11, 2018, accessed January 1, 2020, https://heterodoxacademy.org/the-skeptics-are-wrong-part-2/. Hedges offers a discussion including education in Chris Hedges, *Death of the Liberal Class* (New York: Nation, 2010).

[22] William Stacy Johnson, "Theology and the Church's Mission: Catholic, Orthodox, Evangelical, and Reformed," in *Reformed Theology: Identity and Ecumenicity II: Biblical Interpretation in the Reformed Tradition* (Grand Rapids: Eerdmans, 2007), 67.

[23] The biblical warrant for such an assertion is to be found in the New Covenant in which there is a shift from a more strongly communal witness to the incorporation of individual confession as something of a fail-safe when the institutions of the community have failed. See O'Donavan, *Desire of the Nations*, 80.

[24] J. Brian Tucker, *You Belong to Christ: Paul and the Formation of Social Identity in 1 Corinthians 1-4* (Eugene: Pickwick, 2010), 14.

[25] Ibid.

[26] See Nassim Taleb, *Antifragile: Things that Gain from Disorder* (New York: Penguin Random House, 2012).

[27] Harry Blamires, *The Christian Mind*.

[28] For instance, as much as I enjoy and appreciate some of the individuals identified with the so-called "intellectual dark web," it is important not to mistake what they are doing with the development of a Christian mind. Many of the virtues displayed in conversations between individuals like Jordan Peterson, Sam Harris, Dave Rubin, Joe Rogan, Ben Shapiro, Eric Weinstein and others are commendable, but they are not Christian.

[29] Neil Postman, *Amusing Ourselves to Death: Public Discourse in the Age of Show Business* (New York: Penguin, 2006), xix-xx.

[30] As we enter the world of artificial intelligence (AI), our desires are being anticipated through machines that "learn" what we want, analyze our patterns of life and make convenient habits and behaviors that should perhaps not be reinforced.

³¹ William T. Cavanaugh, *Being Consumed: Economics and Christian Desire* (Grand Rapids: Eerdmans, 2008), 34. For a historical treatment of consumerism, see Frank Trentman, *Empire of Things: How We Became a World of Consumers, from the Fifteenth Century to the Twenty-First* (New York: Harper Collins, 2017).

³² The dynamics that Haidt and Lukianoff describe have the potential to contribute to the dystopian vision of Huxley. For example, Haidt and Lukianoff note, "We suggested that students were beginning to react to words, books, and visiting speakers with fear and anger because they had been taught to exaggerate danger, use dichotomous (or binary) thinking, amplify their first emotional responses, and engage in a number of other cognitive distortions...". Taken to its logical end this dynamic would offer another impetus to stop reading in order to ensure our own comfort. See Jonathan Haidt and Greg Lukianoff, *The Coddling of the American Mind: How Good Intentions and Bad Ideas are Setting Up a Generation for Failure* (New York: Penguin, 2018), 10.

³³ Postman, *Amusing Ourselves to Death*, 155.

³⁴ I would not deny that biblical literacy is an issue about which Christians should have some concern. I do *not*, however, believe that biblical literacy is a root cause. While it represents the more easily visible "tip of the iceberg," there lies beneath the proverbial water an underlying source of the problem. In my estimation, we have biblical literacy less because individual Christians have no interest in the scriptures and more because we do not have a community of faith sufficient to form disciples committed to absolute truth.

³⁵ C. M. Olsen, "Natural Rewards, Neuroplasticity, and Non-Drug Addicitons," *Neuropharmacology* 61 (2011), 14

³⁶ James Clear, *Atomic Habits: An Easy and Proven Way to Build Good Habits and Break Bad Ones* (New York: Penguin, 2018), 27.

³⁷ Ibid., 35.

³⁸ Augustine, *Confessions* 36.59

³⁹ Vivek Wadhwa and Alex Salkever, *Your Happiness Was Hacked: Why Tech is Winning the Battle to Control Your Brain—and How to Fight Back* (Oakland: Barrett-Koehler, 2018), xiv.

⁴⁰ Todd Love, Christian Lanier, Matthias Brand, Linda Hatch, and Raju Hajela, "Neuroscience of Internet Pornography Addiction: A Review and Update," *Behavioral Sciences* 5 (2015), 3-4.

⁴¹ Ibid., 3-4.

⁴² Ibid., 4.

⁴³ Antonius J. Van Rooij and Nicole Prause, "A Critical Review of 'Internet Addiction' Criteria with Suggestions for the Future," *Journal of Behavioral Addictions* 3 (2014),

206.

⁴⁴ Ibid.

⁴⁵ Chip Heath and Dan Heath, *Decisive: How to Make Better Choices in Life and Work* (New York: Currency, 2013), 178.

⁴⁶ Ibid., 115.

⁴⁷ Daniel T. Gilbert and Timothy D. Wilson, "Miswanting: Some Problems in Forecasting of Future Affective States," in *Feeling and Thinking: The Role of Affect in Social Cognition* ed. Joseph P. Forgas (Cambridge: Cambridge University Press, 2000), 178.

⁴⁸ Ibid. 180.

⁴⁹ Ibid., 194.

⁵⁰ Ibid.

⁵¹ In Romans 1, Paul makes a rather clear connection between rebellion and delusion. Denying what is evident in creation and refusing to acknowledge God as Sovereign leads to a "giving over" to the delusion and confusion of "dishonorable passions" and a "debased mind" (Rom 1:18-32).

⁵² Anthony C. Thiselton, *The Hermeneutics of Doctrine* (Grand Rapids: Eerdmans, 2007), 276.

⁵³ Ariana Grande, "7 Rings," track 10 on *Thank U, Next*, Republic, 2019, streaming.

⁵⁴ D.L. Moody, *Morning Devotional* (New Kensington: Whitaker, 2002), 34.

⁵⁵ *Talladega Nights: The Ballad of Ricky Bobby*, directed by Adam McKay (Sony Pictures, 2006).

⁵⁶ Erik Larson, *Naked Consumer: How Our Private Lives Become Public Commodities* (New York: Penguin, 1992), 20.

⁵⁷ In his description of "habit-forming products," Eyal notes, "The fact that we have greater access to the web through our various connected devices—smartphones and tablets, televisions, game consoles, and wearable technology—gives companies far greater ability to affect our behavior" (Nir Eyal, *Hooked: How to Build Habit-Forming Products* [New York: Penguin, 2014], 10-11). He also notes that one of the ways in which these habit-forming products are created is through "variable reward" which "create a craving" (Ibid., 8). Reward variability, according to Eyal, increases the "levels of the neurotransmitter dopamine" and its effects "creating a focus state, which suppresses the areas of the brain associated with judgment and reason while activating the parts associated with wanting and desire" (Ibid., 8-9).

⁵⁸ Jürgen Moltmann, *Theology of Hope: On the Ground and the Implications of a Christian Eschatology* (Minneapolis: Fortress, 1993), 22.

⁵⁹ Joan Chittister, *The Fire in These Ashes: A Spirituality of Contemporary Religious Life* (Franklin: Sheen and Ward, 1999), 105.

⁶⁰ Jürgen Moltmann, "Progress and Abyss: Remembrances of the Modern World," in *The Future of Hope: Christian Tradition Amid Modernity and Postmodernity* ed. Miroslav Volf and William Katerberg (Grand Rapids: Eerdmans, 2004), 22.

⁶¹ *Habitus*, as described by Bourdieu, are "systems of durable, transposable dispositions, structured structures predisposed to function as structuring structures, that is, as principles of the generation and structuring of practices and representations which can be objectively 'regulated' and 'regular' without in any way being the product of obedience to rules, objectively adapted to their goals without presupposing a conscious aiming at ends or an express mastery of the operations necessary to attain them and, being all this, collectively orchestrated without being the product of the orchestrating action of a conductor" (Pierre Bourdieu, *Outline of a Theory of Practice* [Cambridge: Cambridge University Press, 1977], 72).

⁶² Mark A. Noll, *Jesus Christ and the Life of the Mind* (Grand Rapids: Eerdmans, 2011), 152.

⁶³ Ibid.

⁶⁴ Fitch offers a helpful treatment of the church's acquiescence to a variety of "modern maladies" in David E. Fitch, *The Great Giveaway: Reclaiming the Mission of the Church from Big Business, Parachurch Organizations, Psychotherapy, Consumer Capitalism, and Other Modern Maladies* (Grand Rapids: Baker, 2005).

⁶⁵ Taylor, *Modern Social Imaginaries*, 8-9.

⁶⁶ Charles Taylor, "Two Theories of Modernity," in *Alternative Modernities* ed. Filipino Parameshwar Gaonkar (Durham: Duke University Press, 2001), 189.

⁶⁷ Concerning autonomy, Castoriadis notes, "Autonomy is therefore not a clarification without remainder nor is it the total elimination of the discourse of the Other unrecognized as such. It is the establishment of another relation between the discourse of the Other and the subject's discourse. The total elimination of discourse of the Other unrecognized ads such is an unhistorical state" (Cornelius Castoriadis, *The Imaginary Institution of Society* [Cambridge, MA: MIT Press, 1997], 104.

⁶⁸ Blamires, *The Christian Mind*, 189.

⁶⁹ Lukianoff and Haidt, *The Coddling of the American Mind*, 85.

⁷⁰ Ibid., 85-86.

⁷¹ Ibid., 103.

⁷² McConnell's treatment of the application of academic freedom to religious college and universities is quite helpful in addressing the need for a slightly differing conception of

academic freedom within a confessional context (Michael W. McConnell, "Academic Freedom in Religious Colleges and Universities," *Law and Contemporary Problems* 53 [1990], 303-324). Academic freedom aside, it seems to me that there are additional, perhaps more significant, challenges related to the development of non-doctrinal norms that prevent and preclude legitimate biblical and theological inquiry, as well as the labeling of divergent lines of thought as "liberal" or "heretical." These non-doctrinal norms are seldom stated, yet are often weaponized and construed as doctrine in attempt to bring "dissidents" to heel.

[73] Bryan Caplan, *The Case Against Education: Why the Education System is a Waste of Time and Money* (Princeton: Princeton University Press, 2018), 3.

[74] Ibid., 17-18.

[75] Olivier Klein, Russell Spears, and Stephen Reicher, "Social Identity Performance: Extending the Strategic Side of SIDE," *Personality and Social Psychology Review* 11 (2007), 1.

[76] Ibid. 3; it should be noted that out-group sanction does not always create silence or suppress non-normative behaviors. Instead, "behaviours [sic] that are consonant with in-group identity but potentially subject to out-group sanction will be more likely to be expressed when in-group members are visible to each other" (S. Reicher, R. M. Levine, and E. Gordijn, "More on Deindividuation, Power Relations between Groups and the Expression of Social Identity: Three Studies on the Effects of Visibility to the In-Group," *British Journal of Social Psychology* 37 [1998], 17).

[77] Kevin J. Vanhoozer, *Hearers and Doers: A Pastor's Guide to Making Disciples through Scripture and Doctrine* (Bellingham: Lexham, 2019), Loc 385.

[78] Tim Chester and Steve Timmis, *Total Church: A Radical Reshaping Around Gospel and Community* (Wheaton: Crossway, 2008), 18.

[79] Social dynamics and structures constitute something of a two-edged sword. On the one hand, they do serve to police the appropriate boundaries of a community providing shape and continuity to something that might otherwise devolve into chaos. On the other hand, the policing of boundaries and the shaping of communal norms has an impact on individuals, thus creating the potential for limiting diverse viewpoints and creating "static, inflexible, self-centered structures" that "embody a heretical doctrine of the church" (John Stott, *The Living Church: Convictions of a Lifelong Pastor* [Downers Grove: IVP, 2011], 55). It is imperative that the community of faith recognize the sway it has over individuals and the manner in which the self-categorization phenomenon influences individual thought. As Abrams, Wetherell, Cochran, Hogg, and Turner state, "…self-categorization can be a crucial determining factor in social influence, and that the extent of informational and normative influence may depend very largely upon whether the source of influence is regarded as a member of a person's own category" (Dominic Abrams, Margaret Wetherell, Sandra Cochran, Michael A. Hogg, and John C. Turner, "Knowing What to Think by Knowing Who You Are: Self-Categorization and the Nature of Norm Formation, Conformity and Group Polarization," *British Journal of Social Psychology* [1990] 29, 117).

[80] Lee G. Bolman and Terrence E. Deal, *Reframing Organizations: Artistry, Choice, and Leadership* (San Francisco: Jossey-Bass, 2008), 12.

[81] O'Donovan, *Resurrection and Moral Order*, 12.

[82] These three areas are roughly analogous to portions of Berger's and Johnston's work on leadership. See Jennifer Garvey Berger and Keith Johnston, *Simple Habits for Complex Times: Powerful Practices for Leaders* (Stanford: Stanford University Press, 2015).

[83] Scott E. Page, *The Difference: How the Power of Diversity Creates Better Groups, Firms, Schools, and Societies* (Princeton: Princeton University Press, 2007).

[84] Ronald S. Burt, *Brokerage and Closure: An Introduction to Social Capital* (Oxford: Oxford University Press, 2005), 90.

[85] Cass R. Sunstein and Reid Hastie, *Wiser: Getting Beyond Groupthink to Make Groups Smarter* (Boston: Harvard Business Review Press, 2015), 104.

[86] Nassim Nicholas Taleb, *The Black Swan: The Impact of the Highly Improbable* (New York: Random House, 2010), 1.

[87] John Stuart Mill, *On Liberty and the Subjection of Women* (London: Penguin Classics, 2007), 24.

[88] Ormand Rush, *The Reception of Doctrine: An Appropriation of Hans Robert Jauss' Reception Aesthetics and Literary Hermeneutics* (Rome: Gregorian University Press, 1996), 308.

[89] Ibid., 300.

[90] Ibid., 44.

[91] Gary Klein, *Seeing What Others Don't: The Remarkable Ways We Gain Insights* (New York: Public Affairs, 2013), 61.

[92] Berger and Johnston, *Simple Habits for Complex Times*, 17.

[93] Ibid., 18.

[94] Walt Whitman, *The Portable Walt Whitman* ed. Michael Warner (New York: Penguin, 2003), 96.

[95] Thiselton, *The Hermeneutics of Doctrine*, 140.

[96] Ibid., 141.

[97] Ibid.

[98] Berger and Johnston, *Simple Habits for Complex Times*, 39.

[99] Jurgen Habermas, *The Theory of Communicative Action, Volume 1: Reason and the Rationalization of Society* (Boston: Beacon, 1981), 388.

[100] See my discussion of academic disciplines in Bryan C. Babcock, James Spencer, and Russell L. Meek, *Trajectories: A Gospel-Centered Introduction to Old Testament Theology* (Eugene: Pickwick, 2018), 219-229.

[101] Talcott Parsons, *The Social System* (Abingdon: Routledge, 1991), 99.

[102] O'Donovan, *Resurrection and Moral Order*, 14-15.

[103] David J. Snowden and Mary E. Boone, "A Leader's Framework for Decision Making," *HBR* (2007), 5.

[104] Ibid.

[105] Ibid.

[106] Ibid.

[107] Ibid.

[108] These lines were spoken by Darrow, the main character in Brown's Red Rising trilogy, about his mentor whose steely resolve in the face of a world in turmoil was not emulated by his apprentice. Pierce Brown, *Golden Son* (New York: Del Rey, 2015), 247. See also James Spencer "Want to Be a Leader…Make Sure You Have Resolve," Next Generation Christians (blog), January 11, 2019, http://nextgenchristians.com/2019/01/11/want-t0-be-a-leader-make-sure-you-have-resolve/.

[109] Karpicke, for instance, has argued that retrieval practice has significant advantages over other forms of interacting with specific topic areas. Note, for example, his comparison of student use of retrieval practice versus concept mapping on the improvement of test scores in Jeffrey D. Karpicke, "Retrieval Practice Produces More Learning than Elaborative Studying with Concept Mapping," *Science* 11 (2011): 772-775.

[110] Peter C. Brown, Henry L. Roediger III, and Mark A. McDaniel, *Make It Stick: The Science of Successful Learning* (Cambridge: Harvard University Press, 2014), 3.

[111] Ibid., 28.

[112] Ibid., 1.

[113] Samuel Wells, *Improvisation: The Drama of Christian Ethics* (Grand Rapids: Brazil's, 2004), 75.

[114] David E. Fitch, *The End of Evangelicalims? Discerning a New Faithfulness for Mission* (Eugene: Wipf and Stock, 2011), 168.

[115] Clear, *Atomic Habits*, 240.

[116] Ibid.

117 Fitch, *The End of Evangelicalism?*, 169.

118 Maryanne Wolf, *Proust and the Squid: The Story and Science of the Reading Brain* (New York: Harper, 2017).

119 Wolf, *Proust and the Squid*, 3.

120 Ibid.

121 Babcock, Spencer, and Meek, *Trajectories*, 235.

122 Ibid., 237

123 See Eli Priser, *The Filter Bubble: How the New Personalized Web is Changing What We Read and How We Think* (New York: Penguin, 2011); Daniel Kahneman, *Thinking, Fast and Slow* (New York: Farrah, Straus and Giroux, 2013); and Nick Bostrom, *Superintelligence: Paths, Dangers, Strategies* (Oxford: Oxford University Press, 2014).

124 Reading is not necessarily a prerequisite skill for deep engagement. Throughout history, the ability to read the biblical text is a relatively recent phenomenon. Though there are certainly differences between reading a book and listening to a book, there are studies demonstrating that perceived differences between modalities may not impact comprehension. See Beth A. Rogowsky, Barbara M. Calhoun, and Paula Tallal, "Does Modality Matter? The Effects of Reading, Listening, and Dual Modality on Comprehension," *SAGE Open* July-September (2016): 1-9. In addition to the more recent rise in audio books, there is a wealth of literature related to the efficacy of oral tradition. Note, for instance the treatment of oral tradition in Jan Vansina, *Oral Tradition as History* (Madison: University of Wisconsin Press, 1985).

125 Robert P. Waxler and Maureen P. Hall, *Transforming Literacy: Changing Lives through Reading and Writing* (Bingley: Howard House, 2011), 30

126 Sven Birkerts, *The Gutenberg Elegies: The Fate of Reading in an Electronic Age* (New York: Ballantine, 1994), 146.

127 Mikhail M. Bakhtin, "Response to a Question from the Novy Mir Editorial Staff," in *Speech Genres and Other Late Essays* (Austin: University of Texas Press, 2007), 3.

128 Norman Fairclough, *Language and Power* (London: Longman, 2001), 30

129 Ibid.

130 Ibid., 18.

131 I prefer the language of "influence" over control. Fairclough himself notes that descriptions of the relation between discourse and the constraint of social actors "makes social practice sound more rigid than it is" and that "being socially constrained does not preclude being creative" (Ibid., 23-24). The language of "influence" seems to me to denote greater flexibility for social actors to choose to work outside of specific orders of discourse without

denying the persuasive, often unseen, power of those orders of discourse.

¹³² Lillie Chouliaraki and Norman Fairclough, *Discourse in Late Modernity: Rethinking Critical Discourse Analysis* (Edinburgh: Edinburgh University Press, 1999), 21.

¹³³ Mikhail Bakhtin, *Problems of Dostoevsky's Poetics* ed. Caryl Emerson (Minneapolis: University of Minnesota Press, 1984), 69.

¹³⁴ This basic dynamic is being increasingly challenged by the oddly influential forces behind identity politics. Murray offers a helpful critique and commentary on the rapid rise of "identity politics" and its challenges to rigorous dialogue and the pursue of truth in large part because "We are asked to believe things that are unbelievable and being told not to object to things (such as giving children drugs to stop them going through puberty) which most people feel a strong objection to" (Douglas Murray, *The Madness of Crowds: Gender, Race, and Identity* [London: Bloomsbury, 2019], 9). He goes on to note, "The pain that comes from being expected to remain silent on some important matters and perform impossible leaps on others is tremendous, not least because the problems (including the internal contradictions) are so evident" (Ibid.)

¹³⁵ Eli Pariser, *The Filter Bubble*, 124-125.

¹³⁶ Kahneman, *Thinking, Fast and Slow*, 13.

¹³⁷ Daniel Kahneman, "The Marvel and Flaws of Intuitive Thinking: Edge Master Class 2011," in *Thinking: The New Science of Decision-Making, Problem-Solving, and Prediction* ed. John Brockman (New York: Harper, 2013), 395.

¹³⁸ Ibid.

¹³⁹ It may well be that the digital age enhances this tendency given the greater confidence given to us by external sources: "Erroneously situating external knowledge within their own heads, people may unwittingly exaggerate how much intellectual work they can do in situations where they are truly on their own" (Matthew Fisher, Mariel K. Goddu, and Frank C. Keil, "Searching for Explanations: How the Internet Inflates Estimates of Internal Knowledge." *Journal of Experimental Psychology* 144 [2015], 684). It should be noted that the researches admit that similar phenomenon could also occur with non-digital sources (Ibid., 682-683).

¹⁴⁰ Kahneman, *Thinking, Fast and Slow*, 85.

¹⁴¹ Ibid., 23.

¹⁴² I do not wish to advocate for a rejection of all expertise; however, it is important to recognize that simply because a source is trustworthy does not automatically make that source correct.

¹⁴³ Ecker, Lewandowsky, Chang and Pillai demonstrated the impact of framing in "The Effects of Subtle Misinformation in News Headlines" by framing messages about burglary rates through the use of two different headlines addressing a particular situation

within burglary rates (a .2% increase in a given year within a broader decline in burglaries by 10% over the past decade). The two headlines were used to introduce the same article, but one framed the situation in terms of the .2% increase in one particularly year ("Number of Burglaries Going Up") while the other spoke to the broader trend ("Downward Trend in Burglary Rate"). Each headline might be considered "technically true" but those who read the article introduced by the first headline had more difficulty with comprehension prompting Ecker et. al. to recommend informing readers that "editors can strategically use headlines to effectively sway public opinion and influence individuals' behavior. See U.K. Ecker, S. Lewandowsky, E.P. Chang, and R. Pillai, "The Effects of Subtle Misinformation in News Headlines," *Journal of Experimental Psychology: Applied* 20 (2004): 323-334.

[144] While he does not address media in any sustained manner, Sisk Hung Ng's treatment of conversation and power is instructive. See Sik Hung Ng, "Power: An Essay in Honour of Henri Tajfel," in *Social and Group Identities: Developing the Legacy of Henri Tajfel* ed. W. Peter Robinson (Oxford: Butterworth-Heinemann, 1996), 191-214.

[145] Page, *The Difference*, 7.

[146] Garold Stasser and William Titus, "Pooling of Unshared Information in Group Decision Making: Biased Information Sampling During Discussion." *Journal of Personality and Social Psychology* 48 (1985), 1470.

[147] Laughlin distinguishes between intellective and judgmental tasks. The former are those with results that can be objectively evaluated, such as a math problem. The latter do not have clear evaluative criteria by which results can be judged. See P. R. Laughlin, "Social Combination Processes of Cooperative Problem-Solving Groups on Verbal Intellective Tasks," in *Progress in Social Psychology* ed. M. Fishbein (Hillsdale: Erlbaum, 1980).

[148] H. Tajfel and J.C. Turner, "The Social Identity Theory of Intergroup Behavior," in *Psychology of Intergroup Relations* ed. S. Worchel and W.G. Austin (Nelson-Hall: Chicago, 1986), 7-24.

[149] Michael D. Slater, "Reinforcing Spirals Model: Conceptualizing the Relationship between Media Content Exposure and the Development and Maintenance of Attitudes," *Media Psychology* 18 (2015), 380.

[150] Ibid., 375.

[151] Ibid.

[152] Eli Pariser, *The Filter Bubble*, 113.

[153] Note also Google's orientation to "Machine Learning Fairness" in which they offer a general philosophy used to minimize bias in search ("Machine Learning Fairness," Google, https://developers.google.com/machine-learning/fairness-overview). While this sort of search filtering may work well in certain instances, the procedures related to such minimization, particularly latent and selection bias, are problematic. Google's goals in this regard may be noble, however, when they reference the removal of "offensive" and "misleading" information from top-level search rankings or allowing individuals to report

"hateful" or "inappropriate" auto-complete recommendations, there is an assumption that there is some level of agreement about what is or is not offensive, misleading, hateful, or inappropriate. In a society whose historic meta narratives and cultural values are being challenged, Google has the opportunity to do social engineering on an unprecedented scale and with little to no transparency.

[154] To some, the language of reconsidering our fundamental assumptions may well conjure up notions of relative truth or radical deconstruction. There is, however, a difference between intelligible, critical inquiry that remains firmly anchored in the scriptures of the Old and New Testament, thereby recognizing the word of God as a norming norm for life and faith, and the sort of criticism that denies the validity of making any sort of truth claim. As we deal with future generations, it seems to me that we must take care to (a) ensure that the scriptures (not our interpretation of them) remain above reproach and authoritative, (b) recognize the important of the next generation's ownership of the faith (both personally and collectively), and (c) remain open to losing some of what may be good in order to allow the next generation to make its own mistakes…to be incomplete in its own way even as we continue to hold fast to the doctrines and practices crucial to sustaining the faith.

[155] Donald J. Leu, Charles K. Kinder, Julie Cairo, Jill Castek, and Laurie A. Henry, "New Literacies: A Dual-Level Theory of the Changing Nature of Literature, Instruction, and Assessment," *Journal of Education* 197 (2017), 1.

[156] James Paul Gee, *Social Linguistics and Literacies: Ideology in Discourses* 5th Edition (New York: Routledge, 2015), 49. An example of one of the "historically and culturally situated practices" in today's world might involve coding and technological proficiency.

[157] In affirming this aspect of Gee's view, I do not wish to suggest that reading and writing no longer matter or that such skills are not worth fighting to retain regardless of technological advances. Social structures may well influence and shape "new literacies," but it does not follow that we should not be evaluating or even curtailing the use of technology in order to sustain "old literacies" that have enduring (though perhaps a perceived diminished) value within changing social circumstances. The very fact that the ability to read is necessary in order to access much of human history suggests that even if reading and writing become less important in a contemporary context, reading will still be an important skill as long as we place a value on history.

[158] Selecting what information to consume is not limited to internet searching or browsing a bookstore shelf. Developing the capacity to sift information and to evaluate sources, however, has become more challenging as distribution has become less controlled and access more seamless. For a discussion of the processes associated with sifting information see A. J. Flanagin and M. J. Metzger, *An Empirical Examination of Youth Digital Media Use, and Information Credibility* (Cambridge: MIT Press), 2010.

[159] James Davison Hunter, *To Change the World: The Irony, Tragedy, and Possibility of Christianity in the Late Modern World* (New York: Oxford University Press, 2010).

[160] As Weinberg and McCann explain in *Super Thinking*, the various effects of framing, nudging, and anchoring are all part of the broader category of availability bias "which occurs when a bias, or distortion, creeps into your objective view of reality thanks to

information recently made available to you." They go on to note, "Availability bias can easily emerge from high media coverage of a topic." See Gabriel Weinberg and Lauren McCann, *Super Thinking: The Big Book of Mental Models* (New York: Portfolio/Penguin, 2019), 15-16.

161 Mitchell Stephens, *Beyond News: The Future of Journalism* (New York: Columbia University Press, 2014), 148.

162 Murray notes, "As anyone who has lived under totalitarianism can attest, there is something demeaning and eventually soul-destroying about being expected to go along with claims you do not believe to be true and cannot hold to be true" (Murray, *The Madness of Crowds*, 9).

163 The issue of accountability will be addressed more fully in a separate essay; however, I would note that part of the reason that media (social or otherwise) is inadequate to the task of holding leadership accountable is related to a relative lack of depth in our understanding of accountability in the first place. Accountability is not only personal and individual, but structural and communal. We need more serious thought about accountability. Those who address such matters in the media have not, in my estimation, demonstrated the capacity for sufficiently deep engagement in these issues to be a serious part of the solution. While it is likely an overstatement, media tends to steer the angst of the community rather than inspiring deeper thought, particularly when it comes to "crises" facing the Christian community. Without some course correction in this arena, my concern is that what Senator Gracchus says about Rome will become more and more true of the body of Christ, "Rome is the mob. Conjure magic for them and they'll be distracted. Take away their freedom, and still they'll roar. The beating heart of Rome is not the marble of the senate, it's the sand of the coliseum" (*Gladiator*, directed by Ridley Scott [DreamWorks, 2000). Lord, keep us from becoming a people who love the scandal and the kill more than we love each other.

164 There is surely a spectrum of activities in which Christian leaders and ministries might engage that could be classified as lacking full integrity. By using the term here I do not simply intend to denote moral failure, which would represent one extreme along a broader spectrum. Instead, I use "integrity" to denote the effective exercise of one's full resources to the accomplishing of a particular set of tasks or role. Roughly, it means doing the right thing, for the right reason, at the right time, in the right way. As Cloud notes, "When we are talking about integrity, we are talking about being a whole person, an integrated person, with all of our different parts working well and delivering the functions that they were designed to deliver. It is about wholeness and effectiveness as people" (Henry Cloud, *Integrity: The Courage to Meet the Demands of Reality* [New York: HarperCollins, 2006], 31). Ultimately, I would add that Christian integrity is more akin to fitting participation within the community of faith and in relation to God. Such fitting participation would certainly leave room for confession, repentance as acts of integrity.

165 Daniel Kahneman, *Thinking, Fast and Slow* (New York: Farrar, Straus and Giroux, 2011), 203.

166 Kahneman highlights the role of "luck," or what I would refer to as the complex set of factors including divine providence that contribute to success or failure, yet cannot be (or have not been) examined and codified, in the rise and fall of various companies such as Google, "Of course there was a great deal of skill in the Google story, but luck played a more

important role in the actual event than it does in the telling of it. And the more luck was involved, the less there is to be learned" (Ibid., 201).

[167] Coady, *Testimony,* 41.

[168] Ibid., 32.

[169] It seems to me that we are too willing to make the leap from what we see (an observation) to ascribing motive and causality (interpretation). See James Spencer, "What Happens When We Assume Why," Next Generation Christians (blog), March 22, 2019, http://nextgenchristians.com/2019/03/22/267/.

[170] Aside from pointing out that Jesus lost a number of followers when his preaching became too difficult for them to hear (John 6:60-71), current leadership theories also support this conclusion. As Friedman notes, "…the resistance that sabotages a leader's initiative usually has less to do wit the 'issue' that ensues than with the fact that the leader took initiative"(Edwin H. Friedman, *A Failure of Nerve: Leadership in the Age of the Quick Fix* [New York: Seabury, 2007], 3).

[171] Robert W. Jenson, *Systematic Theology*, vol 1: *The Triune God* (New York: Oxford University Press, 1997), 18.

[172] By "transformative discourse" I mean the sort of dialogue that brings people closer together through a greater understanding of one another's thoughts, positions, and perspectives. Such discourse does not necessarily mean that those in conversation will accept one another or that the various participants in a dialogue would end up being united within the same social group. Rather, it is a way of engaging one another that requires strong self-andsocial-differentiation achieved through means other than the demonization of those who are different.

[173] Stephens, *Beyond News*, 142.

[174] It is important to note again here that this essays is not addressing accountability for leaders or organizations. Rather, it is focused on Christian writers and their responsibility to the broader Christian body. As such, the question is not about the shortcomings or immoral acts of others, but about the theologically appropriate means to address present day crises in a digital age. In other words, it is not a question of whether to report or do nothing, thus allowing Christian leaders and organizations to go on behaving badly. Rather it is a question of to what extent mass media reporting is a faithful means of calling Christian leaders and organization to account.

[175] Stephens offers some excellent examples of this sort of reporting. See *Beyond News*, 139-164.

[176] Though it will not be explored in-depth here, there is also the possibility that journalists engage in what Teleb refers to as "naïve interventionism." While there is a genuine intention to help or fix a particular problem, naïve interventions ultimately promotes the fragility of a system or a people. See Taleb, *Antifragile*, 111-120.

177 Hauerwas, *The Work of Theology*, 124.

178 M. A. Hogg and S. A. Reid, "Social Identity, Leadership, and Power," in *The Use and Abuse of Power: Multiple Perspectives on the Causes of Corruption* ed. A. Y. Lee-Chai and J. A. Bargh (New York: Psychology, 2001), 11.

179 M. A. Hogg, and S. A. Reid, "Social Identity, Self-Categorization, and the Communication of Group Norms," *Communication Theory* 16 (2006), 10.

180 It is important to note that prototypicality is not the only factor related to leadership from a social identity theory perspective though it is important both in the emergence and endurance of leaders. Hogg notes social attraction and attribution and information processing as "three core processes that operate in conjunction to make prototypicality an increasingly influential basis of leadership processes as a function of increasing social identity salience…" (Michael A. Hogg, "A Social Identity Theory of Leadership," *Personality and Social Psychology Review* 5 [2001], 188).

181 Who we are will, to a degree, shifts over time. Hogg's analysis of leadership is helpful in that he notes shifts in prototypicality to which sitting leaders must adjust through various means (Ibid., 191). These shifts appear to be occurring in our community now with challenges to consensus norms of a previous era coming from voices both inside and outside the community of faith.

182 Dominic Abrams, Giovanni A. Travailing, Jose M. Marques, Isabel Pinto, and John M. Levine, "Deviance Credit: Tolerance of Deviant Ingroup Leaders is Mediated by Their Accrual of Prototypicality and Conferral of Their Right to Be Supported," *Journal of Social Issues* 74 (2018), 37.

183 Though I cannot prove it, it seems to me that whenever we tie our identity to a particular local institution (e.g. a particular church, organization, academic discipline, etc.), we will be more prone to react in a way that protects that local institution rather than in a way that reflects a broader ecclesiology. Our unwillingness to question whether a given institution should or should not continue creates a situation in which the mission and goals of a given institution become de facto essentials for the gospel in function if not in theory.

184 Take, for example, the "schism" within the Christian community over the endorsement of the "Freedom for All" proposal by the Council of Christian Colleges and Universities (CCCU) and the National Association of Evangelicals (NAE). Despite the pressure from an external lobby, in this case the LGBTQ, the Christian community effectively split over disagreements concerning the tactics used to address the threat in question. Assuming that the reporting is accurate, the endorsement of "Freedom for All" by the CCCU and NAE was framed as "blatantly unbiblical and the exact opposite of 'evangel'—the good news of the gospel" by Everett Piper in the Washington Times (https://www.washingtontimes.com/news/2018/dec/16/how-evangelical-capitulation-equals-the-loss-of-re/). Piper's reaction was not necessarily the norm. While there was a counter movement calling for the preservation of freedom and a rejection of coercion, many of the other objections to the endorsement of the CCCU and NAE focused more on legal matters than on calling out the CCCU's and NAE's decision on theological terms. The point is not to choose a side, but to highlight the dynamics involved in this situation as an example of the

social identity dynamics and how they play out within the community of faith.

[185] Hogg and Reid, "Social Identity, Self-Categorization and the Communication of Group Norms," 22.

[186] Ibid.

[187] J. M. Marques, V. Y. Yzerbyt, and J-Ph Leyens, "The 'Black Sheep Effect': Extremity of Judgments towards Ingroup Members as a Function of Group Identification," *European Journal of Social Psychology* 18 (1988), 4.

[188] M. A. Hogg and R. Martin, "Social Identity Analysis of Leader-Member Relations: Reconciling Self-Categorization and Leader-Member Exchange Theories of Leadership," in *Social Identity at Work: Developing Theory for Organizational Practice* ed. S. Alexander Haslam, Daan van Knippenberg, Michael J. Platow, and Naomi Ellemers (New York: Psychology, 2014), 149.

[189] Hogg, "A Social Identity of Leadership," 188.

[190] While these characteristics are taken from the beatitudes in Matthew, the reference to them as characteristics or identity markers is based on Esler's discussion of the beatitudes in terms of social identity theory. See Philip F. Esler, "Group Norms and Prototypes in Matthew 5:3-12: A Social Identity Interpretation of the Matthean Beatitudes," in *T & T Clark Handbook to Social Identity in the New Testament* ed. J. Brian Tucker and Coleman A. Baker (New York: Bloomsbury, 2016), 147-172.

[191] I address the aspect of permanence and synchronous identity in a later essay. At this point is simply worth noting that, while many of the dialogueues of church history have been recorded (for better or worse), we have entered a new phase of "recording" that is both more permanent and less discerning.

[192] Kevin J. Vanhoozer, *Is There Meaning in This Text?: The Bible, The Reader, and the Morality of Literary Knowledge* (Grad Rapids: Zondervan, 2009), 342.

[193] M. M. Bakhtin, *Speech Genres and Other Late Essays* (Austin: University of Texas Press, 1986), 5.

[194] I will admit that my Facebook feed is not always theologically faithful. In reflecting back on many of my posts, I lament my unreflective surrender to an entertainment culture that dilutes God's greatness by applying the same vocabulary (e.g. "awesome," "great," etc.) to a show, event, or person. My novice Facebook user status doesn't excuse careless posting.

[195] I would not deny that there are "polemics" in Scripture. It seems clear, for instance, that the book of Kings provides a narrative in which one messianic line is authorized over another. These sort of polemics, however, are still theological in nature designed to underscore God's activity amongst his people. Note my treatment of the messianic message of 1 and 2 Kings in Michael Rydelnik and Edwin Blum, *The Moody Handbook of Messianic Prophecy: Studies and Expositions of the Messiah in the Hebrew Bible* (Chicago: Moody, 2019). These polemics,

however, also serve to demonstrate something of God.

[196] Stephens, *Beyond News*, xxvi.

[197] For the concept of the "hyperreal" see Jean Baudrillard, *Simulacra and Simulation* (Ann Arbor: The University of Michigan Press, 1994).

[198] The body of Christ is both visible and invisible. As such, we all have a stake in the way in which individual members of that body or a particular local body of believers behaves. That said, we must take care that our stake in the testimony offered by those with whom we have a relationship largely mediated through consumer mechanisms not contribute to what Jennings calls "the deepest theological distortion" of our day, "that the earth, the ground, spaces, and places are being removed as living organizers and as facilitators of identity" (Jennings, *The Christian Imagination,* 39).

[199] Bahcall makes a distinction between a "system mindset" and an "outcome mindset." Essentially, the pathway or process by which a decision is made is as important as the outcome achieved, whether that outcome is positive or negative. While he discusses the relationship from the perspective of business successes, it seems appropriate to apply a similar logic to the evaluation of the faithfulness of pathways taken to get to a given outcome, whether positive or negative. See Safi Bahcall, *Loonshots: How to Nurture the Crazy Ideas that Win Wars, Cure Diseases, and Transform Industries* (New York: St. Martin's, 2019), 140-144.

[200] Malcom Gladwell, "Small Change: Why the Revolution Will Not Be Tweeted," *The New Yorker* Oct 4, 2010.

[201] Ibid.

[202] Truman's comments regarding the church's treatment of homosexuality are instructive. He notes, "Let me make myself clear at this point: I consider any move by churches to recognize as legitimate the sexual union of homosexual and lesbian partners to be at fundamental odds with the clear teaching of scripture…But, then again, I also consider denial of the resurrection, the trashing of scriptural authority, the mocking of the death of Christ, and the actual trampling of any number of cardinal theological truths also to be at odds with scripture and to be just as pastorally cruel and callous. For me, homosexuality is not the issue; it is rather a symptom of our failure in these other areas; and to treat this as some kind of Rubicon is to misread the signs of the times" (Carl R. Trueman, *The Wages of Spin: Critical Writings on Historic and Contemporary Evangelicalism* (Scotland: Mentor, 2004), chap. 6, Kindle.

[203] Hunter, *To Change the World*, 103.

[204] Ibid., 227.

[205] David E. Fitch, *Faithful Presence: Seven Disciplines that Shape the Church for Mission* (Downers Grove: IVP, 2016), 13.

[206] The terminology of "new" and "old" power is taken from Jeremy Heimans and Henry Timms, *New Power: How Power Works in Our Hyperconnected World—and How to Make it Work for You* (New York: Doubleday, 2018).

[207] Mark Haugaard, ed. *Power: A Reader* (Manchester: Manchester University Press, 2002), 1.

[208] Bertrand Russell, *Power: A New Social Analysis* (London: Routledge, 2004), 23.

[209] Ibid., 4.

[210] Ibid., 8.

[211] Hannah Arendt, *Men In Dark Times* (San Diego: Harcourt Brace & Company, 1968), 22.

[212] Hannah Arendt, *On Violence* (Harmondsworth: Penguin, 1970), 56.

[213] Ibid.

[214] Fairclough, *Language and Power*, 10.

[215] Pierre Bourdieu, *Masculine Domination* (Stanford: Stanford University Press, 2001), 1-2.

[216] Heimans and Timms, *New Power*, 1.

[217] Ibid.

[218] Ibid.

[219] Ibid..

[220] Ibid., 18.

[221] Heimans and Timms refer to this post in Ibid., 81-82.

[222] Moises Naim, *The End of Power: From Boardrooms to Battlefields and Churches to States, Why Being In Charge Isn't What It Used to Be* (New York: Basic, 2013).

[223] David L. Swartz, *Symbolic Power, Politics, and Intellectuals: The Political Sociology of Pierre Bourdieu* (Chicago: University of Chicago Press, 2013), 119.

[224] Naim, *The End of Power*, 17.

[225] Ibid., 52.

[226] Ibid., 13.

[227] Ibid., 229.

[228] Ibid., 236-237.

[229] Applications of social identity theory could inform this reconceptualization of what it means to be the body of Christ even as we exercise "new power." Note, for instance, Esler's treatment of the beatitudes in Matthew in which he concludes, "…the Beatitudes embody group norms expressed in the form of prototypes which are the negation of those of outsiders, and provide evidence for why the identity of the ingroup is the preferable one. The Beatitudes tell the members of Matthew's community who they are and reassure them that they are right to be that way" (Esler, "Group Norms and Prototypes in Matthew 5.3-12," 170).

[230] Hunter, *To Change the World*, 35.

[231] Ibid.

[232] Note that I am not suggesting that there is anything necessarily wrong with being evangelical, conservative, or American. Rather, the challenge is to ensure that one's identification as an evangelical, conservative, and/or American is always a subset…a secondary or tertiary identity…to one's identity in Christ. Our identities, as the research on intersectionality rightly points out, are not monolithic, but are a combination of various characteristics and experiences. As a white, heterosexual, male who grew up as part of the lower middle class in a small rural town in Central Illinois, I see the world differently than other members of the body of Christ. At the same time, my identity in Christ is the controlling identity to which the rest of my characteristics and experiences are subject. I don't lose my unique combination of characteristics and experiences when I come to know Christ, but those characteristics and experiences are no longer ultimately definitive in deciding the course of my life or my inherent character.

[233] J. Kameron Carter, *Race: A Theological Account* (Oxford: Oxford University Press, 2008), 146. While Carter is primarily concerned with race, his comments regarding the issue of "whiteness" point to a dynamic that cannot be solved through simple reversal. In other words, if "blackness" were to replace "whiteness" as the reigning "mythic expression" of Christianity, the body of Christ would surely change, but the dynamics currently associated with "whiteness" would not necessarily be replaced by dynamics more capable of rendering God to the world through the manifold wisdom of the multi-ethnic, highly differentiated body of Christ. Whatever dispositions the body of Christ adopts and whatever *habitus* it develops must be in service not to any one group, but to the ongoing work of serving God as one body without eliminating the contours of local theological wisdoms.

[234] Chris Hedges, *Wages of Rebellion: The Moral Imperative of Revolt* (New York: Nation, 2015), 62-63.

[235] George Will, *The Pursuit of Happiness and Other Sobering Thoughts* (New York: Harper and Row, 1978), 3.

[236] Hunter, *To Change the World*, 35.

[237] A full treatment of Matthew 6 would go beyond the scope of this essay, however, the chapter cautions against making the pursuit of earthly treasure (roughly analogous to "capital" in its various forms) the primary focus of one's life. A fear- and anxiety-driven lifestyle *de facto* calls into question God's ability and/or willingness to provide. Arguably, strategies crafted to pursue God's righteousness or to enact in some manner his kingdom

through the accumulation of some form of capital miss the point by seeking to accomplish God's ends by following a human agenda and using human mechanisms. It is not that God does not position individuals to have means of various sorts with the expectation that they will use the capitals he has granted them for his purposes, but that we misrecognize the state of things when we identify capital as necessary for the work of the gospel.

[238] Oliver O'Donovan, *The Desire of the Nations*, 90.

[239] While focused on idolatry, Benson's work offers a helpful, constructive treatment of certain postmodern movements and theorists. See Bruce Ellis Benson, *Graven Ideologies: Nietzsche, Derrida and Marion on Modern Idolatry* (Downers Grove: InterVarsity, 2002). For discussions regarding epistemology and meaning, see Vanhoozer, *Is There Meaning in This Text?*.

[240] Again, the field of study on oppression is vast. It ranges from "internalized oppression" to more systematized oppression embedded within social structure. For a psychological perspective on oppression see E. J. R. David, *Internalized Oppression: The Psychology of Marginalized Groups* (New York: Springer, 2014). For treatments of systemic oppression see Jim Sindanius and Felicia Pratto, *Social Dominance: An Intergroup Theory of Social Hierarchy and Oppression* (Cambridge: Cambridge University Press, 2001); Safiya Umoja Noble, *Algorithms of Oppression: How Search Engines Reinforce Racism* (New York: New York University Press, 2018); and Simone Weil, *Oppression and Liberty* (London: Rutledge, 1958). Underlying these discussions is the matter of social imaginaries and the inevitable hierarchies they endorse.

[241] The language of "equality of opportunity" versus "equality of outcome" has seen a popular resurgence in large part due to the growing prominence of Jordan Peterson. While there continues to be some utility in maintaining the distinction between opportunity and outcome, it would be an oversimplification to assume that the shorthand slogan "not equality of outcome, but equality of opportunity" reflects the complexities associated with achieving the aspiration conveyed by the slogan. For a critique of the distinction see David A. Strauss, "The Illusory Distinction between Equality of Opportunity and Equality of Result," in *William and Mary Law Review* 34 (1992): 171-188.

[242] See my treatment of Pharaoh's oppression of Israel in Babcock, Spencer, and Meek, *Trajectories*, 65-77.

[243] N. T. Wright, *The Climax of the Covenant: Christ and the Law in Pauline Theology* (Minneapolis: Fortress, 1993), 86.

[244] Ibid., 87.

[245] Kimberlé Crenshaw, "Mapping The Margins: Intersectionality, Identity Politics, and Violence Against Women of Color," *Stanford Law Review* 43 (1991), 1242.

[246] J. D. Vance, *Hillbilly Elegy: A Memoir of a Family and Culture in Crisis* (New York: Harper, 2016), 31.

[247] Pierre Bourdieu, "Social Space and Symbolic Power," *Sociological Theory* 7 (1989), 18.

248 Interests are often viewed as obstacles to be moved aside; however, it is important to recognize the more constructive role of interests as "constitutive of our knowledge, not just (as the Enlightenment believed) obstacles in its path" (Terry Eagleton, "Ideology and Its Vicissitudes in Western Marxism," in *Mapping Ideology* ed. Slavoj Žižek [London: Verso, 2012], 207).

249 Bourdieu, "Social Space and Symbolic Power," 18.

250 Pierre Bourdieu, *Language and Symbolic Power* (Cambridge: Harvard University Press, 1982), 105. Note the similar insight by Berger and Luckmann: "Everyday life is, above all, life with and by means of the language I share with my fellowmen" (Peter L. Berger and Thomas Luckmann, *The Social Construction of Reality: A Treatise in the Sociology of Knowledge* [New York: Anchor, 1966], 37).'

251 It is important to note that (a) Bourdieu draws inspiration from Marxism to the degree that he applies the analogy of economic capital and the notion of power to many different fields and (b) this influence of Marxism can result in overstatements regarding intentionality and domination more generally. Despite this latter challenge, Bourdieu's theories have promise in so much as they do provide a framework for describing a variety of different fields, their hierarchies, and the sorts of *habitus* and capital that would be valued within a given field.

252 Jonathan Auerbach and Russ Castronovo, "Introduction: Thirteen Propositions about Propaganda," in *The Oxford Handbook of Propaganda Studies* ed. Jonathan Auerbach and Russ Castronovo (Oxford: Oxford University Press, 2013), 5.

253 Ibid.

254 Ibid., 2.

255 Eric Weinstein's fourfold typology for fake news (narrative driven, algorithmic, factually false, and institutional), is quite helpful as it expands the notion of "fake" to include matters such as selection, curation, and frequency rather than focusing only on what is "factually false." Weinstein discusses these four types of fake news on the Rubin Report. See Dave Rubin, host, "Eric Weinstein on Fake News, Trump, and the Mathematical Mind," January 6, 2017, accessed January 3, 2020, https://omny.fm/shows/the-rubin-report/eric-weinstein-on-fake-news-trump-and-the-mathemat.

256 Joe Rogan, host, "#1139, Jordan Peterson" Joe Rogan Experience (podcast), July 2, 2018, accessed January 3, 2020, https://youtu.be/9Xc7DN-noAc.

257 Kahneman, *Thinking, Fast and Slow*, 204.

258 Ibid., 199; From a Christian perspective, Kahneman's use of "luck" is obviously problematic. His point, however, is not antithetical to a theological perspective. Ascribing too many effects to human causes or causes brought about through human ingenuity can result in a way of seeing reality that brackets out God. Divine participation or allowance combines with human activity some of which is successful and some of which is not. Judging the God-given

capacities of any individual leader based on God's blessing is a dangerous undertaking.

[259] Ibid., 200.

[260] Ibid., 201.

[261] O'Connor and Weatherall, *The Misinformation Age*, chap. 4. Kindle; The Slave Bible is an excellent, though extreme, example of the manner in which selection of material can skew a message even if everything reported is actually true. See All Things Considered, "Slave Bible from the 1800's Omitted Key Passages that Could Incite Rebellion" produced by Robert Baldwin III and Elizabeth Baker, aired December 9, 2018, on National Public Radio, https://www.npr.org/2018/12/09/674995075/slave-bible-from-the-1800s-omitted-key-passages-that-could-incite-rebellion.

[262] Benson, *Graven Ideologies*, 18.

[263] Ibid., 19.

[264] Ibid., 207.

[265] Hauerwas, *The Work of Theology*, 134.

[266] Benson, *Graven Ideologies*, 81.

[267] Ibid., 49.

[268] Jacob Burckhardt, *The Greeks and Greek Civilization* (New York: St. Martin's Griffin, 1998), 303.

[269] I would liken this phenomenon to that described by Taleb's "naive intervention" which he describes as an "urge to help" and the "harm done by those who intervene." See Taleb, *Antifragile*, 110.

[270] Watzlawick, Weakland, and Fisch offer a slightly different treatment of terrible simplification in which the simplifier denies the presence of a problem and attacks those who name the problem. Such a perspective, while different, is not incommensurate with the view proposed here which sees the identification of a narrow problem (and an accompanying narrow solution) as, in part, a mechanism of denial that leads to attack. In other words, while denial of any problem is certainly one way in which terrible simplification may manifest itself, it is not the only way. See Paul Watzlawick, John H. Weakland, and Richard Fisch, *Change: Principles of Problem Formulation and Problem Resolution* (New York: W.W. Norton and Company, 2011), 40-46.

[271] Valerie A. Brown, John A. Harris, and Jacqueline Y. Russell, *Tackling Wicked Problems: Through the Transdisciplinary Imagination* (New York: Earthscan, 2010), 4.

[272] Daniel Bell, *The End of Ideology: On the Exhaustion of Political Ideas in the Fifties* (Cambridge: Harvard University Press, (2000), 405.

273 See Ben Shapiro, host, "Pastor John MacArthur," Sunday Special Episode 29 (podcast), December 2, 2018, accesssed January 3, 2020, https://podcastone.com/episode/Sunday-Special-Ep-29-Pastor-John-MacArthur. Sunday Special is a long-form podcast that runs for approximately 60 minutes. It is only fair to recognize that it is far more challenging to convey complex ideas in the podcast format. Podcasts are, by design, a bit unstructured and more impromptu and fluid than a theological essay. Because answers are given "in the moment," there is, in my estimation, a higher risk for misstatement.

274 I take this to be an extension of what he notes earlier in the interview when he speaks of the "moral authority" in relation to the Bible.

275 Not all candidates within the Democratic Party are pro-choice, nor are all members of the Republican Party pro-life. While that may well be the general public perception, affirming or denouncing a particular candidate without an assessment of their individual positions is problematic.

276 It should be noted that MacArthur does not explicitly suggest that all Christians should disqualify pro-choice candidates. His overall argument may imply it, but he does not state it explicitly in the interview. That said, his wider influence in certain Christian circles suggests that his personal views, when expressed publicly, may well become an implicit endorsement that Christians adopt those views.

277 Bahcall, *Loonshots*, 142.

278 Ibid.

279 Nancy Murphy, "On the Priority of Personal to Structural Evil in Catholic Social Teaching: A Critique," in *Ethics, Religion, and the Good Society: New Directions in a Pluralistic World* ed. Joseph Runzo (Louisville: Westminster John Knox, 1992), 150.

280 Gutiérrez, *A Theology of Liberation: History, Politics, and Salvation* (New York: Orbis, 1988), 102.

281 Siddharth Kara, *Sex Trafficking: Inside the Business of Modern Slavery* (New York: Columbia University Press, 2017), 3.

282 Stanley Hauerwas, *The Hauerwas Reader* ed. John Berkman and Michael Cartwright (Durham: Duke University Press, 2001), 526.

283 Here it is important to clarify what we mean by "institution." Hierarchies and organization are evident in the early church and described, at least partially, in the scriptures. The institutional aspects in mind here do not preclude such a hierarchy and organization. Instead, the particular mechanisms of the church related to a web presence, church building, utilities, full-time staff, benefits, etc., are all part of the institutionalized church. The institutional aspects of the church are not necessarily "evil," but they are not necessarily permanent either. They are not intrinsic to what it means to be the body of Christ, nor are they essential to the functioning of the church outside of a particular socio-cultural context.

284 This understanding of the church has as its background Pickard's threefold categorization of images of the Church, which include "(a) images concerning connecting and community; (b) images associated with movement and energy; and (c) images concerning the Church's mission and witness in the world" (Stephen Pickard, *Seeking the Church: An Introduction to Ecclesiology* [London: SCM, 2012], 47).

285 Taleb, *Antifragile*, 160.

286 The structure of Matthew 28:19-20 suggest that discipleship (the making of disciples) is to be accomplished through teaching ("...teaching them to obey all that I have commanded you"). Jesus surely did not have formal, accredited education in mind here, but the role of education, or teaching, alongside baptism would seem to suggest that teaching is an aspect of making disciples and that discipleship may be viewed as the end goal of teaching. The Greek constructions here Support such a Reading as "make disciples" is an Aorist imperative upon which the participles "baptizing" and "teaching" are subordinate. For a discussion of the issues surrounding the imperative force of "go" see Benjamin L. Merkle, "Why the Great Commission Should Be Translated 'Go!' And not 'As You G,'" *Southeastern Theological Review* 9.2 (2018): 21-32.

287 My line of argument here is not intended to suggest that I think it is time to move away from higher education completely. After an eleven year career as a higher education administrator an ongoing ministry serving as an adjunct faculty member, I continue to see the necessity of the sort of learning and credentialling that higher education is uniquely designed to provide. At the same time, higher education as an industry has its problems and we must, as a community of faith, be wise not to authorize or support any initiatives designed to preserve the higher education status quo. Such initiatives tend to assume that everyone should earn a degree, which suggests as subtle dismissal of working class jobs that do not require degrees.

288 Kevin J. Vanhoozer and Daniel J. Treier, *Theology and the Mirror of Scripture: A Mere Evangelical Account* (Downers Grove: IVP, 2015), 99.

289 Thomas R. Schreiner, *1 Corinthians: An Introduction and Commentary* (Downers Grove: IVP, 2018), 266.

290 Thompson, *Hit Makers*, 185-208.

291 Regarding culture Davidson suggests that the capacity to define "what is good, bad, right, wrong, real, unreal, important, unimportant, and so on…is not evenly distributed in a society, but is concentrated in certain institutions and among certain leadership groups who have a lopsided access to the means of cultural production." He also notes, "Culture change is most enduring when it penetrates the structure of our imagination, frameworks of knowledge and discussion, the perception of everyday reality…Change of this nature can only come from the top down." See Davidson, *To Change the World*, 41-42. Such a reading of the capacity to change culture minimizes the impact of individuals and grass roots movements to create and sustain meaningful change. Hedges' work offers some counterpoints to Davidson's more pessimistic views on grass roots change. See Chris hedges, *Wages of Rebellion: The Moral*

Imperative of Revolt (New York: Nation, 2015).

²⁹² Pickard, *Seeking the Church,* 185.

²⁹³ Ibid.

²⁹⁴ I recognize that for some the theological position is itself problematic being viewed as a remnant of patriarchal culture that needs to be rooted out of the church. For an insightful navigation of the issue of women in the church see Carolyn Custis James, *Half the Church: Recapturing God's Global Vision for Women* (Grand Rapids: Zondervan, 2015).

²⁹⁵ G.K. Chesterton, *The Collected Works of G.K. Chesterton* vol. 3k (San Francisco: Ignacio's, 1990),157.

²⁹⁶ Huizinga, "A Definition of the Concept of History," 6.

²⁹⁷ Schreiner, *1 Corinthians,* 65-66.

²⁹⁸ For a full treatment of 1 Corinthians 1-4 from the perspective of social identity see Tucker, *You Belong to Christ.*

²⁹⁹ Slavoj Žižek, *The Sublime Object of Ideology* (London: Verso, 1989), 102.

³⁰⁰ Fitch, *The End of Evangelicalism,* 46

³⁰¹ Ibid.

³⁰² *Braveheart*, directed by Mel Gibson (Parmount Pictures, 1995).

³⁰³ Wells, *Improvisation,* 12.

³⁰⁴ Taleb, *Antifragile,* 110-113.

³⁰⁵ Ronald A. Heifetz, *Leadership without Easy Answers* (Cambridge, MA: Harvard University Press, 1994), 22.

³⁰⁶ Ibid., 7.

³⁰⁷ Ibid., 2.

³⁰⁸ Ibid.

³⁰⁹ There is little difference between the argument made by most prominent evangelicals who advocate for a return to the Judeo-Christian ethic and that made in Ben Shapiro, *The Right Side of History: How Reason and Moral Purpose Made the West Great* (New York: Broadside, 2019). It is not that I necessarily disagree that the United States might be better off if its citizens were to return to a moral vision more akin to the Judo-Christian ethic. My contention, rather, is that there is a gap between the moral trajectory of the United States and the theological trajectory of the church. For Christians living in the United States, the two are

surely intertwined; however, the fact that they are intertwined does not make them of equal value.

[310] Anthony C. Thiselton, *First Corinthians: A Shorter Exegetical and Pastoral Commentary* (Grand Rapids: Eerdmans, 2006), 90.

[311] Faith and Leadership, "Stanley Hauerwas: What Only the Whole Church Can Do," December 21, 2009, video, https://faithandleadership.com/multimedia/stanley-hauerwas-what-only-the-whole-church-can-do.

Made in the USA
Monee, IL
30 January 2020